MILES M.52

GATEWAY TO SUPERSONIC FLIGHT

T0244438

MILES M.52

GATEWAY TO SUPERSONIC FLIGHT

Captain Eric Brown CBE DSC AFC QCVSA RN
in association with Dennis Bancroft C.Eng MRAeS

The
History
Press

The 1:48 scale model of the M.52 which appears
on the title-page was built by Keith Sherwood
and presented to Dennis Bancroft.

First published 2012
First published in paperback 2022

The History Press
97 St George's Place, Cheltenham,
Gloucestershire, GL50 3QB
www.thehistorypress.co.uk

British Library Cataloguing in Publication Data.
A catalogue record for this book is available from the
British Library.

ISBN 978 1 80399 167 2

Design and production by Blacker Limited
Printed and bound in the EU on behalf of Latitude Press

Contents

List of appendices

Foreword

This is a book that tells the inside story of what should have been for Britain a supreme triumph in the annals of aviation – the breaking of the sound barrier to attain supersonic speed in a piloted aircraft, but it was not to be.

The standard bearer for this venture was the Miles M.52 research aircraft, arising from an exceptionally brief specification issued in 1943 by the Ministry of Aircraft Production, and assigned, to the astonishment of many, to one of Britain's smaller aircraft manufacturers, but one with a reputation for innovatory thinking. However, as a safeguard the project was to be monitored by the Royal Aircraft Establishment at Farnborough (RAE), which would also provide a test pilot with wide jet flying and transonic flight testing experience.

Well, they always say if you want something to fall into your lap, you've got to be in the right place at the right time. It just so happened that I was a young, but fairly experienced, test pilot in the Aerodynamics Flight and the High-Speed Flight at RAE in 1944, when I was told I was nominated to be the RAE's pilot for the M.52 project.

I realised I could only discuss this within a very limited circle, as the project was classified TOP SECRET, and this new circle contained some very senior figures in British aviation and politics. Although the majority of these showed strong support for the project, there was a hard core who had genuine concerns about the high risks associated with it.

However, a new factor cast its shadow over the project – the intrusive interest of the Americans, with the full support of the British Government. The American interest was understandable, because the M.52 had some very innovatory features – a bi-convex wing, an all-moving tailplane (flying tail), a pilot escape capsule and a revolutionary jet engine designed by Frank Whittle. From this point the M.52 story began to assume the nature of a conspiracy, and indeed one that today remains unsolved.

The dénouement was the tragic cancellation of the M.52. This drastic action was totally unheralded, caught everyone in the project team absolutely by surprise, particularly as the aircraft was over 90% completed to flight status. For me this meant deep disappointment, total frustration, burning anger, and heartfelt sympathy for other members of the team. For our proud nation it meant betrayal of our leading position in high-speed flight technology.

Acknowledgements

I wish to acknowledge the assistance given to me in the writing of this book. In particular Dennis Bancroft, Peter Amos (The Miles Aircraft Collection) and Josh Spoor. Each of them has devoted many years to researching the mystery of the cancellation of the contract for the aircraft which would have ensured that Britain was the first nation to break the sound barrier.

As Chief Aerodynamicist on the M.52 Dennis Bancroft is in an unique position to confirm the technical details of the plane's innovatory design, which Miles conceived in a remarkably short time. His wife, Elizabeth, has been invaluable in searching out and assembling the relevant papers.

Extra information has come from Jeremy Miles, son of F.G. and 'Blossom' Miles, from Jean Fostekew (Museum of Berkshire Aviation), Jim Pratt, George Miles' son-in-law, Rod Kirkby.

Professor Brian Brinkworth's paper 'On the aerodynamics of the Miles M.52 (E.24/43) – a historical perspective' in *The Aeronautical Journal* of the Royal Aeronautical Society is a wonderful technical assessment of the Miles' achievement; his conclusion is that 'Miles made an astute appraisal of the available information, and conceived a forward-looking machine, that was well fitted for its intended purpose ... the most plausible estimates of available thrust and drag would indicate that sonic speed would not be exceeded in level flight, though speeds well into the supersonic range would be obtained in a dive. An opportunity to acquire a promising and most timely research tool was lost in its cancellation'.

The chronology of events on pages 173 to 212 was researched by Elwyn Blacker.

Abbreviations

A&AEE	Aircraft and Armament Experimental Establishment, Boscombe Down
AD/ARD	Assistant Director, Armament Research Department, MoS
AM	Air Ministry
ARC	Aeronautical Research Committee
ARD	Armament Research Department
CRD	Controller of Research and Development, MAP
DAF	Directorate of Aircraft Factories
DARD	Director of Aircraft Research and Development, MoS
DD/RDA	Deputy Director, Research and Development Administration, MAP
DDSR	Deputy Director of Scientific Research, MAP
DFS	German Research Institute for Glider Flying
DGP	Director General of Production, MoS
DGSR	Director General of Scientific Research, MAP
DGTD	Director General of Technical Development, MAP
DSP	Director of Special Projects, MAP
DSR	Directorate/Director of Scientific Research, MAP
DTD	Directorate/Director of Technical Development, MAP
GTTACC	Gas Turbine Technical Advisory and Coordinating Committee
ICAN	International Commission for Air Navigation
MAP	Ministry of Aircraft Production
MoS	Ministry of Supply
NACA	National Advisory Committee for Aeronautics (US)
NGTE	National Gas Turbine Establishment
NPL	National Physical Laboratory
RAE	Royal Aircraft Establishment, Farnborough
USAAF	United States Army Air Force
USAF	United States Air Force

1 In the beginning

Sub-Lt (A) Eric Brown
RNVR, in 1940.

The winning Supermarine
Schneider Trophy S6B
seaplane, 1931.

One of the main catalysts to arouse man's interest in high-speed flight was the Schneider Trophy series of air races for seaplanes, which took place between 1913 and 1931. The influence of this competition can be gauged from the fact that the first winning speed was 61mph and eighteen years later the last race was won at 340mph.

By coincidence, in the first six months of 1928, the year sandwiched between the first and second of the three victories that gave Great Britain outright possession of the Schneider Trophy, a 19-year-old cadet named Frank Whittle at RAF Cranwell was writing his required fourth term science thesis entitled 'Future Developments in Aircraft Design'. In that remarkable document Flight Cadet Whittle postulated the possibility of flight at 500mph in the stratosphere where the air density was less than one-quarter of its sea-level value. To meet the power plant needs of such a high-speed/high-altitude aircraft, young Whittle discussed the possibilities of gas turbines driving propellers, but not the use of the gas turbine for jet propulsion; in the latter field he was shortly to lead the world.

In winning the Schneider Trophy, Britain's greatest asset was not just to be the international prestige it gained, but the nurturing of the genius of R.J. Mitchell, the young designer who worked for the Supermarine division of Vickers-Armstrong Ltd, and was mainly responsible for the superb designs of the S4, S5, S6 and S6B, the latter three being the winning seaplanes in the years 1927, 1929 and 1931. The full potential of these racing machines was shown on 29 September 1931 when the S6B, fitted with a special 'sprint' engine, raised the World's Speed Record by more than 40mph, to 407.5mph. With war looming on the horizon Mitchell went on to develop his Schneider Trophy masterpieces to the pinnacle of the most famous military piston-engined fighter of all time, the Rolls-Royce Merlin engined Supermarine Spitfire, which made its maiden flight on 6 March 1936.

R.J. Mitchell, designer of Britain's Schneider Trophy winning seaplanes and the incomparable Spitfire.

Frank Whittle, by now a qualified RAF pilot, filed his patent for a jet propulsion engine on 16 January 1930 and it was granted in October 1932. This was all done without any scientific, moral or financial support, and although the Air Ministry was notified it expressed no official interest in the patent. So there was no suggestion that Whittle's patent should be put on the secret list, and his invention could be published openly throughout the world.

In spite of the frustrations of the next four and a half years, Whittle succeeded in getting his first test engine running on 12 April 1937, but there were difficulties still ahead.

With the prospect of war coming ever closer there was frantic activity in the fighter manufacturing field, mainly represented in Great Britain by the Hawker Aircraft Company's Hurricane and Supermarine's Spitfire. Fortunately both products were available to participate in the Battle of Britain, and were a revelation in their handling characteristics, firepower and particularly their performance attributes.

The Royal Aircraft Establishment at Farnborough (RAE) was heavily involved in promoting the advancement of fighter performance and in October 1941 initiated a programme of tran sonic flight testing with a Spitfire Mark V.

The Mach numbers that could be attained by this aircraft were somewhat limited by its operating ceiling, but were of the order of 0.75 to 0.78. Excitingly enough, although these goings on were highly classified, new words like 'compressibility', 'sound barrier' and 'supersonic' began to appear in aviation magazines and even be heard in crew-room discussions.

Squadron Leader
J.R. Tobin, who was
CO of Aero Flight
at RAE Farnborough
in 1942.

1. Until 5 October 1943
the company was
Phillips and Powis
Aircraft Ltd.

By a twist of fate I was shortly to meet Squadron Leader J.R. Tobin, who was CO of Aero Flight at RAE Farnborough where he was involved in the new programme of transonic testing. At the same time I was to learn something of the innovatory reputation acquired by Miles Aircraft Ltd,[1] located at Woodley, near Reading.

I had first met a Miles product when I carried out my elementary flying training in 1939 for the Fleet Air Arm on the Miles Magister, which I found a delight for such a task. This story now jumps to 21 December 1941, when I was a pilot flying Grumman Wildcat fighters aboard the escort carrier HMS *Audacity*, which was sunk by a German U-boat in the Bay of Biscay. I was subsequently on survivor's leave, when I was recalled by Admiralty telegram to report to the RAE Farnborough to fly the Miles M.20 to assess its suitability as a possible fleet fighter.

I arrived at the RAE on 5 January 1942 and was handed over to Sqn Ldr Tobin, who had been assigned to show me over the M.20, bearing the Serial No. DR616. My first impression was of something that looked a sort of cross between the Hurricane and Spitfire, with a smaller wing span and a more pugnacious nose than either. However, its two striking features were the fixed undercarriage and the bubble type cockpit hood, the latter to become commonplace in fighters, but at that time a rare innovation. The aircraft was of wooden construction and powered by a Rolls-Royce Merlin XX engine.

Tobin showed me over the cockpit layout and said I should familiarise myself by flying it for about an hour, and then he would join me in a Hurricane for a spell of dogfighting.

In essence my report to the Admiralty expressed the view that the M.20, although surprisingly nippy in performance, could not match the Wildcat, Hurricane or Spitfire for manoeuvrability and did not offer enough speed performance over the Wildcat or Hurricane to give an offsetting advantage. However, my biggest misgiving was whether the wooden airframe could withstand the punishment of shipborne operations.

I was reasonably impressed with the M.20, but more so with the Miles design team when Tobin told me the aircraft was designed, built, and flown in 65 days, this being made possible by using Miles Master trainer standard parts, the elimination of hydraulics, and the fitting of a fixed undercarriage. The concept was to offer a fighter capable of speedy production if we suffered heavy fighter losses in the Battle of Britain. Indeed the M.20 had some very attractive advantages in that it could carry $12 \times .303$ Browning machine guns in the wings, 5,000 rounds of ammunition, and 154 gallons of fuel – virtually double the fire power and endurance of the Hurricane and Spitfire. These hard facts convinced me of the innovative expertise of the Miles team.

Although at that time I knew nothing of Tobin's involvement in transonic flight testing, just to make conversation over lunch I asked him what he made of the popular subject in aviation journals of the possibility of breaking the sound barrier in the future. He shrugged his shoulders and said that some boffins believed it could not be done, and that was certainly so of propeller-driven

The Miles M.20 with its innovative bubble cockpit canopy.

Britain's first jet aircraft, the Gloster/Whittle E.28/39. It undertook a comprehensive test programme at RAE Farnborough between March 1944 and February 1945.

aircraft because of the drag of the propeller, but most felt it would be possible with jet or rocket-powered aircraft.

This gave me great food for thought, because by sheer chance I had witnessed the maiden flight of Britain's first jet, the Gloster E.28/39, at Cranwell airfield on 15 May 1941, although I did not appreciate what it was at that time.

It happened like this – I was in 802 Squadron, equipped with Grumman Martlet (Wildcat) fighters, at Royal Naval Air Station Donibristle in the shadow of the Forth Bridge, and we were working up for our first operational assignment. But American designed aircraft had only a lap strap for pilot safety restraint and this was not deemed sufficient for arresting deceleration on an aircraft carrier. Modification was arranged to fit a full shoulder harness, but for this to be done each pilot had to fly his aircraft to Croydon airport, outside London.

I took off for Croydon on 14 May 1941 and ran into very bad weather near Lincoln and was lucky to creep into Cranwell before it clamped down. To my amazement the officers' mess was alive with dozens of civilians, all looking and acting like conspirators, and I was roomed with a Flight Lieutenant Geoffrey Bone, who unknown to me was one of Frank Whittle's team and indeed was the installation engineer for the jet engine in the E.28/39. He would not be drawn on what was afoot. Indeed it was not till the evening of the next day when the weather improved slightly that I saw the strange propellerless machine for the first time as it was wheeled out of the hangar and finally took off with a whistling noise for a short flight. On landing it was greeted by an RAF officer who was obviously a key player in whatever was going on. This then was my introduction to a machine I was eventually to test fly three years later at Farnborough, and to a man of genius who was the true inventor of the practical jet engine and with whom I was to enjoy an amicable working and social relationship for many years.

Today, when I look back on these past events, I get a strange sense of predestiny – 802 Squadron Wildcats; the E.28/39 historic first flight and the presence of Frank Whittle; flying the innovative Miles M.20 at Farnborough; meeting Squadron Leader Tobin who was to pioneer transonic flight testing at RAE. To my mind there is a clear line of connection running through those events which had an inevitability, culminating in my association with the Miles M.52 supersonic research project.

A rare view of the Gloster E.28/39 being flown by Eric Brown on its last flight on 20 February 1945.

2 A big step into the unknown

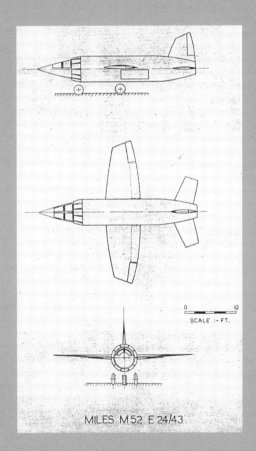

One of the first outline design drawings of the M.52, produced by Miles Aircraft.

MILES M 52 E 24/43

SCALE :- FT.

0   10

My first official appointment as a test pilot was in mid-1942, at about the same time as the magnificent Spitfire Mark IX burst upon the aviation scene. This aircraft, with its two-stage supercharged Merlin engine, arrived at a crucial point in time to provide the increase in performance to match the ubiquitous Focke-Wulf 190, but also to allow the RAE's Aero Flight to expand the scope of its transonic flight testing into Mach numbers of 0.80 and above.

The phenomenon of compressibility in connection with such work was now more fully understood. An aircraft in flight sends pressure waves ahead of it which part the air and let it through. At lower speeds this air has time to get out of the way, but at speeds approaching the speed of sound this can no longer happen. The air which was previously following the streamline around the aircraft now hits it directly and a wall of compressed air builds up ahead of it until it forms a barrier, which has to be pierced to attain supersonic flight. The amount of power required to break the sound barrier is considerable.

Compressibility effects show themselves in various ways, most generally by heavy vibration escalating into severe buffeting, followed by an increasingly powerful nose-down change of trim. This may need a two-handed pull to counteract it, or the use of a trim flap which if activated will effect a nose-up change of trim. This is a highly dangerous phase of flight testing and in combat operations has caused many fatalities.

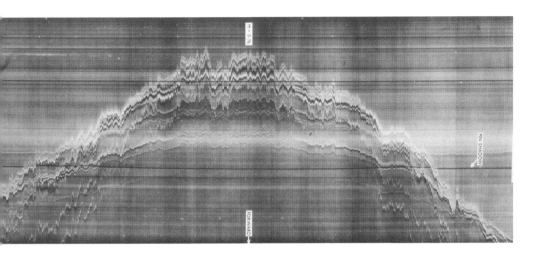

Shadowgraph of a compressibility shock wave on the wing of a Vampire at 540mph at 2,000ft, taken at dusk in April 1948 at RAE Farnborough.

It was at this stage in the RAE's transonic flight test programme that the boffins felt confident enough to make plans for a supersonic research aircraft. They drew up specification E.24/43, which must be the shortest ever issued by the Ministry of Aircraft Production (MAP):

1. Design and develop a new fast Research Aircraft powered by a W.2/700 + No. 4 Augmentor Whittle engine with bypass heating

2. An all-up weight between 5,000 and 6,000lb.

3. Target speed 1,000mph.

4. Enough fuel to climb to 40,000ft plus ½ hour at 700mph.

5. Monoplane with large tailplane, the tailplane to be all-moving, i.e. no elevator.

6. Target date 9 months hence.

This specification was presented at an MAP meeting on 9 October 1943 to which F.G. Miles had been invited, and at which he was offered the chance to meet it. He was astonished at the target speed of 1,000mph, but did not wish to jeopardise the offer by

F.G. Miles learned to fly in the 1920s. In 1932 he went into partnership with Phillips and Powis to build light aircraft and became Technical Director and Chief Designer. He later took over the firm and it became Miles Aircraft, with his brother George as Technical Director.

querying this requirement. Research intelligence emanating from Germany had indicated that they were developing a high-speed aircraft:

> 'The cruising speed of this aircraft is about 1,300kph (800mph) and its maximum 1,800kph (1,000mph) at a height of 18,000 metres. It should be able to fly from Berlin to New York in about three hours.'

Miles was now expected to submit a quick preliminary outline design of how the company envisaged meeting Specification

E.24/43. Norbert Rowe, Director of Technical Development (DTD) at MAP, visited Miles at Reading on 6 November 1943 and was impressed by the design layout he was shown so that he proposed to Air Marshal Sir Ralph Sorley, Controller of Research and Development (CRD), the placing of a contract for two prototypes and parts for a third. This was agreed on 15 November 1943, and placed with Miles Aircraft on 13 December 1943 'as a matter of urgency', although it was actually dated 29 December 1943.

In close aviation circles the award of the contract to Miles Aircraft Ltd of the world's first supersonic research aircraft caused some consternation, for the company was hardly regarded as being in the big league of aircraft manufacturers. Long renowned for the design and construction of elementary and advanced training aircraft, Phillips and Powis Aircraft Ltd as the firm was known until 5 October 1943 – when the name was changed to Miles Aircraft Ltd – had never ventured into the tricky territory of high-speed aerodynamics. However, they would be strongly supported by the RAE scientists and facilities such as wind tunnels.

The reasons for the choice of this small company for such a vital project were three-fold. Primarily it was Hobson's choice, for all the major aircraft manufacturers were at full production capacity to meet the demands to provide operational aircraft in the middle of a desperate war. Secondly, Miles had gained a reputation for innovative design as shown in the M.20 fighter and M.26L X.11 transport aeroplane. Thirdly, the company's headquarters, factory and airfield were located at Woodley, on the outskirts of Reading, and reasonably near to Farnborough, thus making contact liaison with the RAE quite easy.

Once F. G. Miles had been slotted into this unique MAP project he wasted no time in springing into action. A fearsome challenge in the field of high-speed aerodynamics now faced the Miles team, and particularly for Dennis Bancroft, its Chief Aerodynamicist. To find the latest information on the subject a visit was made to Ronald Smelt of the Aerodynamics Department of the RAE. Dennis Bancroft now recounts the saga of the pursuit of transonic/supersonic enlightenment in Chapter 3.

Miles M.26L X.11, a drawing of the projected transport.

3 A steep learning curve

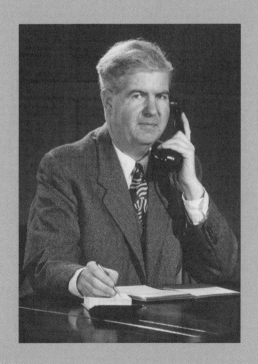

Dennis Bancroft was
Miles Aircraft's Chief
Aerodynamicist. He was
responsible for the
M.52's aerodynamics.

To find the latest information on the subject, a visit was first made to Ronald Smelt of the Aerodynamics Department of the Royal Aircraft Establishment (RAE), Farnborough. He informed us that the RAE had no supersonic wind tunnels, and the highest wind speeds they could test were quite a way below the speed of sound, but they were showing the very rapid increase of drag at their maximum speeds of about Mach 0.8. He explained that the RAE had no method of measuring transonic drag as yet, but until one was found he thought that something like a 10- to 20-fold increase in drag was likely to be encountered, although the actual drag might well fall somewhat as the speed increased to over – say – Mach 1.1 or so.

This was why Smelt thought that there was very little likelihood of achieving anywhere near the 1,000mph with the latest Whittle engine.

Ronald Smelt said that though there was very little knowledge of transonic drag, a very thin wing and small frontal area of a fuselage would be essential. They had made a preliminary estimate of a small, thin winged aircraft and, even for quite different drag estimates, always came out with a maximum level speed of about 600mph. Even doubling the thrust from Whittle's engine would only increase the maximum level speed by 10 to 20mph, as the expected subsonic drag was assumed to rise so rapidly. Diving the aircraft would increase its speed, but not sufficiently to reach Mach 1.0. A design with a high ceiling appeared necessary, to give a slightly higher maximum speed in the dive.

We left the RAE rather depressed, as the information provided only confirmed the then general impression of the aircraft industry that the 'sound barrier' was impregnable to all, and Whittle's engine was not nearly powerful enough to accomplish the job!

But all this pessimistic information was not based on any actual measurements of the conditions to be encountered, but only on extrapolation of data to an unknown area. Also, if this 10- to 20-fold drag increase was believed by the MAP, why should they be considering giving Miles Aircraft a contract for an impossible job?

The next visit was to the Aeronautical Department of the National Physical Laboratory (NPL), Teddington, to meet Ernest Relf and Dr Hilton, and an entirely different approach to supersonic flight was found. They had also been given details of the Whittle engine, and thought the project to reach 1,000mph realistic, but by no means easy.

The NPL had three supersonic wind tunnels working. The largest had a working section of 12 inches in diameter, but even that required so much power that it could only be run in the early hours, before 5a.m. The type of induced flow meant that the tunnel ran at one speed only, and major parts would have to be changed to obtain another speed. The tunnel models were usually bodies of revolution, in connection with ballistic work on bullets and shells at higher Mach numbers, and a model of a complete aircraft had never been tested. While they would be most interested in testing such a model, and could measure the drag and pitch forces, they would have no idea of tunnel correction, but comparing flight tests of the aircraft itself with the model tests would be most useful for the future.

Referring to information on supersonic aircraft design Ernest Relf recommended Ackeret's *Theory of Aerofoils Moving at Speeds Greater than that of Sound*, as explained by Taylor in R & M 1467, published in 1932 and available to the public since then for about 3s. 6d. He said the simple theory of this report had been remarkably accurate for the applications it has been used for, and the lift and drag produced by this theory is reasonably correct. A range of other reports were shown, such as that giving Busemann's theory[1] covering second order terms, etc.

The available reports gave a real working set of theories to enable one to produce a realistic supersonic aircraft with reasonable confidence of the results. But – all this information applied only to stable supersonic flight above a Mach number of about 1.25. There were no reports or data for the transonic flow. Normal subsonic theories produced data up to – say – Mach 0.8 to 0.85, and entirely different theories provided what was thought to be accurate data from Mach 1.25 upwards. But what happened between Mach 0.85 and Mach 1.25 was another matter! Both subsonic and supersonic theories were completely wrong at Mach 1.0.

One factor was known about this region, and that was that the centre of lift for a lifting wing below Mach 0.8 was at approximately 24% of the chord,[2] and at Mach numbers over 1.25 it had moved to approximately 50% of the chord. When this movement takes place – and how fast – was completely unknown.

Neither the NPL nor RAE had any method of finding what really happened in the transonic region. None of the wind tunnels could be run in this region and, when trying to increase or decrease speeds to this area, shock wave reflections and other unknown tunnel corrections completely defeated the obtaining of practical results.

I asked Ernest Relf if he had any idea of the magnitude of the drag increase at about Mach 1.0 or so, because the RAE thought it to be enormous, with a factor of about 10 or 20, but really could not give any good reason for this figure.

Ernest Relf's opinion was that, although there was probably a small 'bump' of drag increase when passing through the speed of sound, it must be much less than that from his knowledge of ballistic experiments where bullets and shells had been fired

1. Adolph Busemann was a German aerodynamicist, who was considered a leading authority on wing sweepback.

2. Chord is the distance between the leading edge and trailing edge of the wing.

and drag measured for many years and only small drag increases had been recorded. Of course, most of the work was on bodies of revolution and not lifting wings, but the order of the drag results should be similar. He recommended a visit to Dr Maccoll of the Armament Research Department (ARD) at Fort Halstead, where practical testing of ballistics was organised and a vast amount of transonic and supersonic data was collected. Dr Maccoll could probably give more information on the change of drag of a body of revolution throughout the speed range, as well as recommending shapes for bodies of minimum supersonic drag.

The plan view of a supersonic aircraft was discussed, and several alternatives considered. The smallest frontal area and very thin wings were, of course, essential, but Busemann, for example, had suggested at the Volta Congress of High Speed in Aviation, at Rome in 1935, that swept-back wings could reduce the onset of higher supersonic drag. He later describes a supersonic biplane, where the shock waves would theoretically cancel themselves out to a certain extent.

It was thought that a delta layout might, in time, be the most efficient for speeds of about Mach 1.5 and over, but would need years of development. The swept-back wing would be the best platform to 'nudge' into the sound barrier, but only if the maximum speed was Mach 1.2 or so. For a speed of Mach 1.5 the orthodox plan was preferable, as there would be fewer 'unknowns' and, provided there was sufficient engine thrust, a satisfactory outcome was more certain. The use of a bi-convex wing section might be necessary.

Ernest Relf said that it was obviously a compromise between what one knew and how far one might be pressed into the unknown to produce a satisfactory solution. He had used Whittle's engine to produce a supersonic design, and to reach Mach 1.5 had used a small wing of aspect ratio of 3. I did think the lateral control at take-off and landing with such a small span might not be acceptable, but to increase the span would increase the drag.

Dr Busemann at Farnborough in 1947.

The NPL produced a great deal of information on supersonic flight, with much of the data confirmed by experiment, but little about the transonic region. They recommended Dr Maccoll as the only real source of practical transonic knowledge.

On Sunday, the 17 October 1943, the Miles design team paid a visit to Power Jets at Brownsover, to discuss the supersonic project with Frank Whittle and his design team. The operation of the proposed special jet engine was described, but only a rough overall drawing was so far available. We would have to provide for a tubular engine, approximately 3ft in diameter and 18ft long, chiefly filled with flame at about 1,500° absolute (1,227°C). In particular, there could be no aircraft structure or controls, etc., passing through or across this 18ft long tube. The weight of the basic W.2/700 engine was given as 850 to

Front view of W.2/700 engine.

900lb plus the No. 4 Augmentor at 300lb and the remaining ducting at 100lb.

The static thrust of the basic W.2/700 was now 2,000lb but a 25% increase was expected by next year, with the use of new turbine materials able to run at higher temperatures.

The existing W.2/700 plus No. 4 Augmentor unit was expected to give about 5,000lb thrust at 1,000mph at 36,000ft, and this was expected to be increased next year in a similar manner.

Diagram of proposed special jet engine as propulsion unit for M.52.

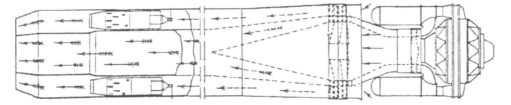

Rear view of W.2/700 engine.

M.52 power plant being prepared for test at Whetstone.

Air Cdre Frank Whittle.

M.52 power plant running under test at Whetstone on 3 July 1945.

On showing Frank Whittle our first ideas on the general layout of the aircraft, which was much like the final design built, he immediately brought up his idea of considering the Busemann biplane layout and, instead of the all-moving tailplane, considered moving the angle of one complete wing relative to the other for longitudinal control of the aircraft.

We were silently horrified at the idea, as our principle was to incorporate as much as possible of current knowledge and minimise the unknown. And there was still plenty of 'unknown'! We discussed the magnitude of using such a theoretical layout and the problems of just the low-speed flight, let alone transition and supersonic flight. We also pointed out that the specification required 'a monoplane with large tailplane, the tailplane to be all-moving'. We expressed our opinion of our layout and that, provided a bi-convex wing would behave reasonably well at low speeds, the overall design should achieve the required 1,000mph, but would probably need to dive through the speed of sound. Any increase in the supersonic thrust from the engine would be welcomed.

The general discussion on the aircraft was left at that, and we went to Whetstone to see various jet test beds and a W.2/700 being started and run.

A visit to Dr Maccoll at the ARD at Fort Halstead in late October provided an insight into the vast amount of projectile data available for transonic and supersonic speeds. The majority of course, was for solids of revolution travelling at these speeds. The effect of shape was well documented.

The drag of bullets and shells followed a somewhat similar shape, with the fall of speed typically from the maximum launch speed at high Mach number. The drag reduced steadily with speed to – say – Mach 1.1, then fell more rapidly to perhaps half to a quarter of the drag when the speed had fallen to Mach 0.9. No high peaks, as suggested by the RAE, were ever found. In fact, where the RAE were saying they thought an increase in drag from Mach 0.9 to 1.2 was some 10- or 20-fold,

Dr Maccoll's data all showed an increase over the same speed range of only 2- to 4-fold. Dr Maccoll did emphasise, however, that frontal area was so much more important for transonic and supersonic speeds than subsonic ones. For example, supersonic drag increases roughly in proportion to the square of the thickness of the wing, compared to the square root of the thickness at subsonic speed.

Dr Maccoll confirmed the NPL's general statement that the drag of a body was expected to be greater by a factor of 2 to 4 between a Mach number of 0.9 and 1.1, due principally to pressure waves, and many actual measurements confirmed this. He completely disagreed with the RAE's thoughts of a 10 to 20 times increase. These high figures were just not borne out by measured results for thin sections.

We were now much more confident that the project was at least possible, and presumed that the Ministry had been accepting Dr Maccoll's actual measurements rather than the RAE's out-of-date theories! With this remarkably large quantity of theoretical and practical measurements, both in the supersonic and transonic regions, we were able to produce a preliminary design.

By using a thin, bi-convex wing and an orthodox plan form, and relatively high take-off and landing speeds, we produced an aircraft which would probably meet all the specified requirements, including the 1,000mph in level flight. But it was just not possible in only nine months!

Just four weeks after Miles was first approached, on 6 November 1943, Norbert E. Rowe of the Directorate of Technical Development (DTD) with other MAP and Power Jets personnel, visited Miles Aircraft at Woodley, to judge what progress had been made, and whether Miles had produced a satisfactory aircraft design to meet the specification.

Miles recommended their preliminary design, which, incidentally, looked very much like the final design.

It was pointed out that while a delta plan form had both drag and structural potential advantages for supersonic speeds, the lack of any low or high-speed data would mean years of research before a successful delta aircraft could be designed with confidence.

While a wing with a small sweepback would reduce the drag over a small range around the speed of sound, it would have no advantage at 1,000mph unless a sweep of 55° to 60° was used, and then all the unknown problems of the delta wing would have to be faced.

The proposed layout was such that most of the problems could be solved with present-day knowledge, with the exception of whether satisfactory low-speed performance could be obtained from a bi-convex wing section. As there was absolutely no information on this section at normal speeds, a 7½% thickness/chord wing had already been rapidly made and tested in the Miles wind tunnel, and a satisfactory flow and stall had been obtained, suggesting that the bi-convex section could be used.

However, a full-scale flight test needed to be made as soon as possible, in particular to check the low speed characteristics. It would also be very desirable to fit the all-moving tailplane, both for aerodynamic measurements and to give pilots some feel and confidence with this control.

Of course, one other agreement on data was essential for any form of aircraft to exceed about 600mph in level flight, and that was to accept that the RAE's 10- to 20-times drag increase between Mach 0.85 and 1.15 was, in fact, incorrect, and the ballistically measured 2- to 4-times increase was nearer the true figure. On this basis, the Miles design should achieve the 1,000mph target, but might have to dive shallowly to pass through the sound barrier.

On returning to the Ministry Norbert Rowe wrote a very positive note saying: 'The firm have evolved a very attractive layout. I think the firm has shown, by the way they have tackled the initial stages, that we could safely entrust this project to them' (Appendix 2).

He suggested, therefore, that a contract should be placed on Miles Aircraft Ltd for two prototypes and parts for a third. The contract was duly awarded for the aircraft, to Specification E.24/43, dated 13 December 1943.

One unexpected problem was that the project was classified MOST SECRET. This meant that one could not use the telephone, and while letters could be sent, special non-GPO (General Post Office) methods had to be used which slowed up transfer or, apparently, never reached the correct person at all.

Here Captain Brown continues with the story:

When I first learnt of the M.52's bi-convex wing I longed to get a second opinion on its effectiveness other than that of the Miles/RAE team. My opportunity came just after the end of World War II when the Farren Mission[1] brought a number of selected German aeronautical scientists to the RAE for interrogation. One of these was Dr Adolph Busemann, the world's leading authority on wing sweepback.

I queried with him whether we had made the right wing choice for supersonic flight with the M.52. He replied that his area of expertise was mainly in the transonic flight region, but he had learned a lot about supersonic flight from two of his co-workers, Dr Jacob Ackeret, a Swiss aerodynamicist who worked at the Aerodynamic Research Establishment at Göttingen during World War II, and Antonio Ferri, an Italian who in 1939 conducted tests on thin aerofoils, including a bi-convex, at speeds up to M=2.13 in the high-speed tunnel at Guidonia in Italy. Apparently both Ackeret's and Ferri's analysis of these tests favoured the bi-convex aerofoil for supersonic flight.

1. In early 1945 the Ministry of Aircraft Production set up the Farren Mission, named after W.S. Farren, Director of the RAE Farnborough, to seek out the aviation advanced technology secrets in post-war Germany. The Mission was comprised of RAE scientists and test pilots.

4 The Supersonic Committee

The Me 163A starting
its take-off run at
Peenemünde.

This MAP committee arose out of a meeting held on 4 May 1943 to consider an intelligence report based on interrogation of a German prisoner of war. The report indicated that the Germans were developing high-speed aircraft capable of 1,000mph (1,609km/h), and it almost certainly refers to the flight of the Messerschmitt 163A third prototype on 2 October 1941, when Flugkapitän Heini Dittmar broke the 1,000km/h barrier. Dittmar, a test pilot for the German Research Institute for Gliding (DFS) at Darmstadt was assigned to fly for Dr Alexander Lippisch, the designer of the Me 163, which developed into an operational rather than a research aircraft.

A second meeting of the Supersonic Committee held on 4 June was largely concerned with information from enemy sources, but action was taken to initiate tests of ram-jets and rockets at supersonic speeds.

At its meeting in November 1943 the Committee first considered a piloted supersonic aircraft. This was to be the Miles E.24/43, which had knife-edged wings and tail surfaces and was to be powered by a Whittle gas turbine with reheat.

By this time the Committee was fully established and was meeting monthly to consider methods of achieving speeds equal to, or greater than, that of sound. It initially comprised 19 members from 15 different ministry departments and 4 private companies, and this total was gradually expanded with a further 11 new members. Surprisingly no representative from Miles Aircraft Ltd was ever invited, and indeed the company

Heini Dittmar, Germany's foremost rocket-propelled aircraft test pilot in World War II.

The Supersonic Committee Chairman, Ben Lockspeiser, Director of Scientific Research (DSR).

did not even know of its existence. The Committee Chairman was Ben Lockspeiser, Director of Scientific Research (DSR).

The Supersonic Committee was classified as TOP SECRET, and this meant that a considerable amount of wildly inaccurate information and data was circulated at these meetings from time to time – unchallenged and uncorrected.

Of course, the specific members present, though experienced in their own fields, naturally had no experience of the design and construction of a supersonic aircraft, and no way of comparing the data put before them with what might feasibly be realistic. For example, on the very erroneous drag estimates from the RAE which were repeatedly circulated, the first one reported in the minutes of Supersonic Committee Meeting No. 8

on 14 December 1943, was criticised in detail by Julian Hodge of Power Jets, and his report of 3 January 1944 makes interesting reading:

> There appears to have been some confusion about the RAE performance estimates. Those referred to initially are those obtained before our visit to Mr Smelt, when the thrust estimates which the RAE had were very much lower than those finally given. The RAE have stuck to their certainty of what the drag will be at supersonic speeds and give the top speed as 600mph, while there is in fact quite a reasonable chance of getting to 1,000mph.
>
> There is also a misapprehension about the ultimate wing thickness to be aimed at. We understand from Miles Aircraft that this is 4% not 5%.
>
> It is said – 'In order to operate at great heights to permit diving, fuel consumption must be kept as low as possible, otherwise the ceiling would be limited by the amount of fuel that can be carried'. In fact the rate of climb of this aircraft will be so large that the fuel used in the climb will be quite a small amount, especially at altitudes above 40,000ft. The ceiling will probably be somewhere between 60 and 70,000ft.
>
> The sentence – 'The necessity for high operating altitudes also renders it essential that the wings must operate successfully at low Mach numbers' is a reversal of the facts, since the higher the operating altitude, the higher will be the climbing speed.
>
> Mr Smelt says we intend to use temperatures up to 1500°C, meaning 1500° Absolute presumably (*sic*).
>
> Dr Griffith's[1] reference to the necessity for a variable exhaust nozzle is of course covered by the fact that it is possible to control the gas angles in the fan either by varying the nozzle size or the bypass combustion temperature; we are doing it by the latter means.
>
> Landing at full wing loading should be unnecessary, especially in view of the fact that a jettisonable tank is carried.

1. Dr A.A. Griffith was Head of the Engine Section of the RAE Farnborough. He was also a member of the Supersonic Committee.

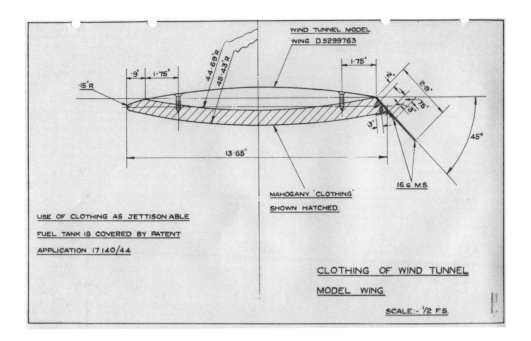

Drawing of the jettisonable wing fuel tanks. Initially it was thought these would be necessary to reach operating altitudes.

The wing structure appears to be chiefly the concern of Miles Aircraft.

The whole basis of the scheme is that we have always realised that it would be necessary to dive the aircraft through the speed of sound, but this has not appeared to be too much of a snag since the aircraft will have a very high ceiling. Everyone seems much too confident of the accuracy of the RAE supersonic drag estimates, as when this meeting was held, Dr Maccoll, who was the only person who could be of any great help in this respect, had not examined the scheme in detail. He has since told us that the data used by the RAE, especially that relating to scale effect, is very badly wrong. Hence, until we receive his estimates, we have nothing at all reliable to go on.

It is significant that the Power Jets representative made this important contribution, because Power Jets Ltd was a private company formed by Frank Whittle and partners in March 1936 and this showed its interest in the Miles E.24/43 was very much alive. Indeed, at this point in time Whittle, who was to provide the W.2/700 engine with afterburning in both the jet and in a surrounding bypass flow, was developing two forms of turbofan – which he called thrust augmentors – which gave increased thrust by burning additional fuel before and after the fan turbine.

Thus the end of 1943 finished with a flurry of activity surrounding the new supersonic research aircraft which the Miles company had now named the M.52 and which presented a titanic challenge ahead.

Whittle with the Power Jets team in 1945. Julian Hodge is on the far left of the group.

5 In at the deep end

The four pilots of the
Aerodynamics Flight.
From left to right:
Sqn Ldr Tony Martindale,
Sqn Ldr Jimmy Nelson,
the author and Sqn Ldr
Doug Weightman.

W hen the momentous wartime year of 1944 dawned I was a test pilot at the Aircraft and Armament Experimental Establishment (A&AEE), Boscombe Down. But not for long as fate stepped in and I was hurried on my way to RAE Farnborough to replace a pilot killed in the course of his test work. This was an unexpected promotion for me, as RAE was the country's top aviation research centre. Furthermore, when I arrived there on 17 January I found myself destined for the prestigious Aerodynamics Flight, which also incorporated the High-Speed Flight and the Jet Flight. It was for me a dream come true.

Aero Flight was an élite group of only four pilots, of whom three formed the High-Speed Flight, and a supernumerary ran the Jet Flight. I found myself within four months in all three units, because the CO Experimental Flying, the senior test flying administrator at RAE, decreed that the Navy must have equal

Left: W.S. Farren, Director of the RAE at Farnborough.

Right: Morien Morgan, Head of Aero Department Flight Section and controller of the flight test programme for Aero Flight at Farnborough.

representation with the RAF. In those four months I think I must have learned of every TOP SECRET aviation project alive in Britain, but no mention at all of the M.52.

There was intense flying activity in Aero Flight, particularly in transonic flight testing, using Spitfires IX and XI and American Lightning, Thunderbolt and Mustang fighters. In the Jet Flight we had the Gloster E.28/39 and Meteor, the de Havilland Spider Crab, later to be renamed Vampire, and the Bell Airacomet. All very exciting, and to add to the excitement Frank Whittle was a frequent visitor to the Jet Flight for obvious reasons.

Then out of the blue came a bit of super excitement when on 4 August 1944 I received a handwritten note from Mr W.S. Farren, Director of the RAE, saying: 'I would like you to start taking a close interest in the supersonic research programme being conducted by RAE in conjunction with Miles Aircraft Company. To this end you should liaise with Morien Morgan'. The latter was Head of Aero Department Flight Section and controlled the flight test programme for Aero Flight. Since I saw Morien almost on a daily basis, and he flew quite often as my flight test observer, this was a perfect situation for me, and I soon heard of the existence of the M.52 for the first time.

This was the start of frequent visits with Morien to Miles Aircraft at Woodley, where we had meetings with the key figures there, and viewed progress on the mock-up of the M.52. Morien told me to pay special attention to the cockpit proposals as the intention was that I would make the first flight and the initial transonic and supersonic research flights. This may sound rather like walking over the Miles chief test pilot's head. But the hard facts were that only one of the Miles test pilots was small enough to get into the restricted cockpit dimensions of the M.52; neither had flown jet aircraft nor had any experience of transonic flight testing.

Although this may seem a unique situation, it was to be repeated in the case of the Boulton Paul P.111 delta research aircraft and the Handley Page H.P.115 slender delta wing slow

M.52 fuselage mock-up
at Woodley in 1945.

speed research aircraft. In both cases the initial flights were undertaken by the CO of RAE's Aero Flight.

My initial interest in the M.52 mock-up centred on the nose cone pilot escape capsule, which was protruding from the annular air intake to the jet engine. The maximum diameter of this capsule was only 5ft and the pilot was housed in the cockpit in a semi-reclining position. In the event of an extreme emergency the pilot would activate the escape system which would fire four explosive bolts, thus detaching the nose cone by impelling it forward from the aircraft. When free, a drogue parachute would deploy from the capsule to slow it down and

the pilot could then make a normal bale out, using his own parachute. The system seemed perfectly feasible to me, but to allow more time to develop it the decision was eventually made to fit it on the second prototype only, as this was the one that would carry out the attempts to fly supersonic.

The pilot escape capsule was not the only feature that impressed me on my first visit to Woodley, for there was also the bullet-like fuselage, the bi-convex wings, and the air intake arrangement for the mighty jet engine. But perhaps it was the calm confidence of the Miles team that left me with a positive feeling that we were on a winner with the M.52.

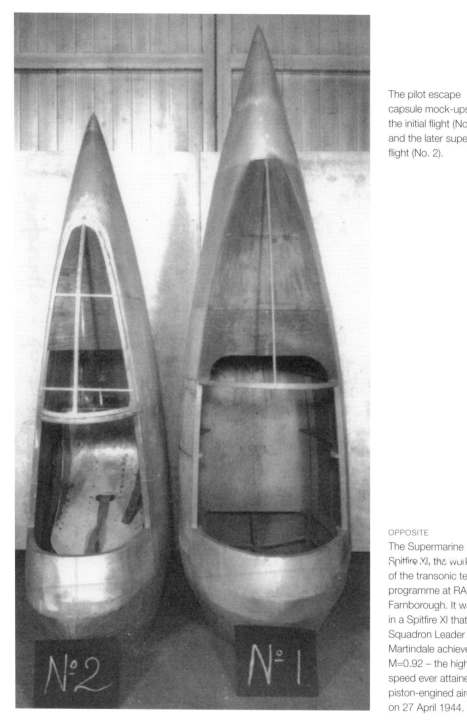

The pilot escape capsule mock-ups for the initial flight (No. 1) and the later supersonic flight (No. 2).

OPPOSITE
The Supermarine Spitfire XI, the workhorse of the transonic testing programme at RAE Farnborough. It was in a Spitfire XI that Squadron Leader Tony Martindale achieved M=0.92 – the highest speed ever attained in a piston-engined aircraft – on 27 April 1944.

Squadron Leader
A.F. Martindale, CO of
Aero Flight at RAE in
1944–5.

Encouraging news had arrived that two W.2/700 engines had been installed in a Meteor and test flown in April. Meanwhile, Whittle was seeking to perfect his No. 4 thrust augmentor.

The prospect of supersonic flight, even before we knew anything of the M.52, seemed to act like an injection of adrenalin into the Aero Flight pilots. In our transonic tests with the Spitfire PR XI, which carried no armament to disturb the smooth contours of the wings, I attained a Mach number of 0.88 true, which was the limit of my physical strength to control the nose-down forces imposed by compressibility effects.

However, better was to come. On 27 April 1944 Squadron Leader Tony Martindale achieved M= 0.92 in the same Spitfire XI. This is the highest speed ever attained in a piston-engined aircraft, and was due in no small measure to the pilot's physical attributes – 6ft 2in tall and weighing 210lb.

6 The Gillette Falcon

The Miles M.3B Falcon Six, Serial No. L9705, before the Gillette modifications.

B y early 1944 the Miles team had formed a firm opinion, as a result of its deliberations with ARD, that the fuselage shape of the M.52 should take the form of a 0.5-calibre bullet.

However, the selection of the wing was a more complex matter, because not only did the aerofoil section have to be selected, but the span determined and a decision made whether to go for a sweepback or a straight wing. Since the M.52 was not intended to be marginally supersonic, but take a big bite of the supersonic cherry and aim for at least Mach 1.5, it was preferable to use a bi-convex straight short-span wing where fewer unknowns would have to be coped with. The decision to go for the bi-convex section was influenced by the Swiss aerodynamicist Ackeret's *Theory of Aerofoils Moving at Speeds Greater than that of Sound.* This report had been available to the public since 1932.

Obviously the other essentials needed to meet the objective were a very thin wing and a lot of engine power; the thinness of the wing would have considerable effect on the take-off and landing characteristics of the aircraft. The inevitable answer to finding out more about low speed handling was to construct a flying test bed with a symmetrical bi-convex wing, and Miles made a 7½% thickness/chord wing and tested it in their own wind tunnel. A satisfactory flow and stall was obtained. The next material progression was to make a full-scale flight test to let pilots get the feel of the controls.

A Miles M.3B Falcon Six, Serial No. L9705, that had been supplied to RAE in April 1938 for full-scale flight tests on experimental wings Miles had made, was returned and fitted with a wooden bi-convex wing. This wing differed slightly from the M.52 in having straight leading and trailing edges, an area of 160sq ft, a root thickness of 7½% and tip thickness of 5½%. It had razor-sharp leading and trailing edges, together with a narrow tracked undercarriage attached directly to the fuselage in order to keep the wing free of all excrescences, but it would have split flaps on the trailing edge of the wing. Because of the sharpness of its wing the aircraft became known as the Gillette Falcon. Removable guards were fitted to the wing to protect the engineers after one had cut his head open through accidentally walking into it.

On 11 August 1944 the modified aircraft was flown by Miles company test pilot Flt Lt Hugh Kennedy, who reported good lateral control and smooth stalling characteristics.

After many hours of flight testing, including actually measuring the full-scale wing lift and drag, the Falcon standard tailplane and elevator were replaced by a thin bi-convex tailplane and elevator, which were fitted at Farnborough in mid-November 1944. Flying recommenced at Woodley later that month.

A symmetrical bi-convex wing aerofoil section was chosen with its thickest point at 50% chord, as being structurally easier than a simple double-wedge aerofoil which had theoretically better supersonic drag characteristics. Structurally the wing was to all intents solid, being attached to the fuselage frames behind the engine such that the incidence setting of the wing could be changed on the ground. In plan form the wing was almost elliptical, but with tips cut off diagonally along the line of the outer shock wave. The whole wing was thus designed to be within the V-shaped shock wave from the nose of the aircraft (Appendices 2 and 3).

Many flying hours with the Gillette Falcon had produced reports by the Miles pilots showing satisfactory low speed performance of the bi-convex thin wing and that good lateral control was achieved with good stalling characteristics. These reports seemed a little too cosy to me, especially as in the case of the M.52 so thin a wing had never been attempted in Britain before. I suspected that such a wing would have 'flat plate' qualities that might produce at higher angles of attack, as for landing, an uncontrollable rate of sink.

However, there came a new and extremely vital factor into the M.52 equation. The RAE thought Miles was providing too small a tailplane as a result of tests made in the RAE high-speed 11ft tunnel, and suggested it be increased by 10%. Miles was not happy with this as it was already 32% of the gross wing area and gave adequate stability. But they agreed to do it, as the disadvantages of the added pilot's control load and the increased weight of the reserve hydraulic pneumatic reservoir, to give the same emergency control capacity for when the power failed, would probably be worth it. Additionally the improvement

OPPOSITE

Top: The Gillette Falcon, fitted with the bi-convex wing.

Below: The Gillette Falcon, fitted with the bi-convex wing and all-moving tailplane (flying tail).

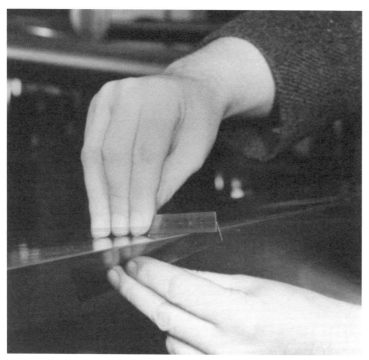

The razor-edge thinness of the bi-convex wing is demonstrated.

 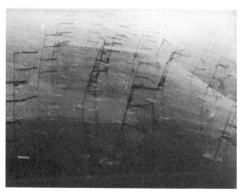

Top: The Gillette Falcon cockpit on test at Woodley.

Below: Surface wool tufts to delineate airflow patterns on the Gillette Falcon.

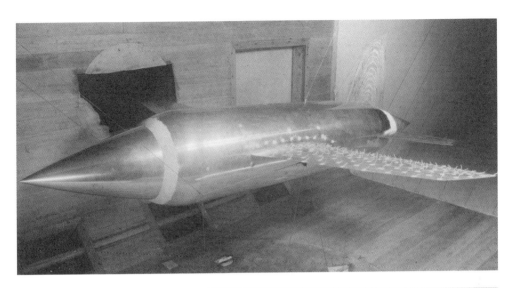

Top: Scale model of the M.52 with compressed
wood wing on test in Miles wind tunnel.

Below: Model of the M.52 used for testing in the
RAE wind tunnel, see model II in Appendix 10.

offered for dealing with an emergency landing would make the increase in all-up weight acceptable to get the added security provided by the larger tailplane in the unknown transonic and supersonic regions. On 27 September 1944 a Spitfire IX, Serial No. PV290, having an increased area tailplane which may, it is understood, have been manufactured by ML Aviation of White Waltham, arrived at RAE where I conducted tests on it between 27 October and 4 December 1944 up to Mach 0.86. I found it improved control effectiveness in recovery from transonic dives.

In early 1945 the Falcon was fitted with the all-moving tailplane, and flying then recommenced in late February. About this time too a series of other wind tunnel tests was being conducted with models of the M.52. A one-thirty-sixth scale model with solid steel wing and tail surfaces was made for the NPL 12-inch supersonic wind tunnel. This approximately 9-inch span

Tests being carried out in the NPL 12-inch supersonic wind tunnel.

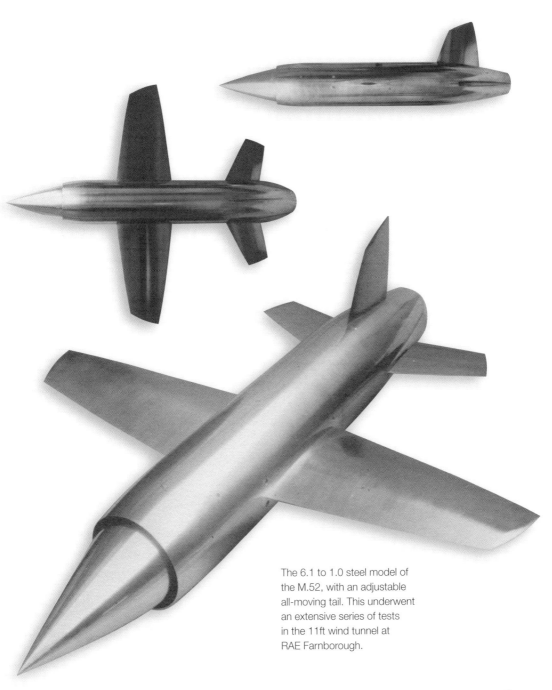

The 6.1 to 1.0 steel model of
the M.52, with an adjustable
all-moving tail. This underwent
an extensive series of tests
in the 11ft wind tunnel at
RAE Farnborough.

model was tested at Mach numbers of 1.45 and 1.25 for drag and pitching moments. The NPL, however, did specifically explain that those tests should be considered for general interest and not for accurate indication of full-scale drag estimates, etc., as there were absolutely no full-scale tests of any wing body configuration for comparison. Undoubtedly, reflected shock waves in the tunnel would seriously affect the results in a manner so far unpredictable.

The initial tests were made in a metal working section where shock waves could not be seen, so Miles Aircraft made a special Perspex working section to run at Mach 1.45 and show the actual shock waves produced and reflected around.

A 6.1:1.0 scale model of the M.52, with a compressed wood wing, was made and tested in the Miles wind tunnel, while a stronger, solid steel wing and tail unit were made to be tested in the RAE high-speed subsonic 11ft tunnel (see Appendix 10). I witnessed these latter tests for myself, and it was quite awe-inspiring to see the behaviour of the shock waves, or 'gremlins' as we called them, in the transition from subsonic to supersonic flight. It was in some ways a sobering experience to realise we were entering unknown territory and I was under no illusion about the risks involved, but I was satisfied that my destiny would be in the hands of a superb team.

Morien Morgan and I regularly continued to have meetings with the Miles team at Woodley, consisting usually of the Miles brothers, Don Brown, Dennis Bancroft, Lionel 'Toby' Heal, and occasionally Ken Waller, Hugh Kennedy or Blossom Miles, F.G.'s very aeronautical wife. These meetings were very informal and because of the high classification of the M.52 project no minutes were kept, at least not to my knowledge. They usually concluded with a walk around a mock-up of the M.52, and I never ceased to get a great thrill in seeing the vision being gradually created and dreaming in my mind of its incredible potential.

George Miles became Technical Director of Miles Aircraft Ltd. An experienced pilot, he often made the first flights in aircraft designed by the firm.

7 A fateful visit

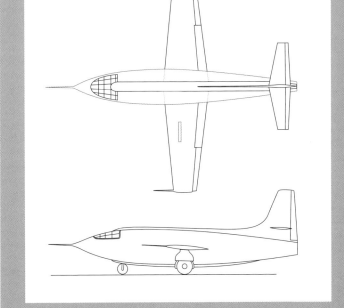

Drawing of the Bell X-1, highlighting the straight wing, almost certainly influenced by the American visit to the Miles' factory.

In the autumn of 1944 the MAP arranged a visit to Miles Aircraft by a number of Americans representing the United States Army Air Force (USAAF), the National Advisory Committee for Aeronautics (NACA) and Bell Aircraft Corporation. On the instructions of the MAP, Miles was to give the visitors all the information on the M.52 and answer their questions, and in three weeks time it was hoped a reciprocal visit to the USA would be made by a Miles design team and a similar full exchange of information on American supersonic flight knowledge would take place.

To understand the American desire for the visit to Miles, it must be remembered that in 1944 the Germans and the British were ahead of the rest of the aviation world in high-speed research. With the end of World War II in sight the Americans wanted desperately to get on the leader board in the race to supersonic flight. We probably responded wholeheartedly in a gesture of gratitude to our gallant ally, and fully accepted the reciprocal offer in good faith. Here we came unstuck, however, because one week after the American visit the MAP told the Miles team that the return visit had been cancelled by the Pentagon for security reasons. It is much more likely that the US visitors had been taken aback by what they had learned in the UK and wished to save themselves the embarrassment of having to admit they had little to offer.

The United States did not have the development history capable of producing the powerful kind of jet propulsion system required to break through the sound barrier, so veered towards the brute force of rocket propulsion, although this imposed some severe operating limitations in terms of flight endurance and thrust control for the pilot. Also the USA did not have the wind tunnel facilities to conduct the range of aerodynamic research required to prepare for supersonic flight. In these respects it was Hobson's choice – seek all the help you can get and initiate a series of practical full-scale high-speed flight tests on what were to be the American X-planes.

On 16 March 1945, some six months after the visit to Miles, the USAAF launched its formal supersonic aircraft programme by awarding a contract to Bell Aircraft Corporation for three rocket-powered aircraft to be built to USAAF specifications but with the technical inputs from NACA. Shades of the Miles Aircraft and RAE partnership. By that time the war in Europe was in its final stages and the Americans were relying heavily on the spoils of war in the German field of rocketry.

Eventually it had hardly come as a surprise to learn that the Bell Experimental Sonic-1, or X-1 as it came to be known, had a fuselage based on a 0.5-calibre bullet. It also had a straight thin wing (but not as thin as that of the M.52, nor with the razor-sharp leading edge[1] of the M.52's bi-convex supersonic wing section), and tail-plane adjustable in incidence for trim purposes, with a conventional trailing-edge elevator. There was something all very *déjà vu* about this to my critical eye, except for the horizontal tail, but that was yet to change.

1. A similarly sharp leading edge was later chosen by Lockheed's Kelly Johnson for the Mach 2 F-104 Starfighter, also with straight, rather than swept, wings. The leading edges had to be fitted with protective covers on the ground to prevent ground crews from serious injury!

Bell pilots completed the contractor's flight demonstrations by 5 June 1947, and then the USAAF took over and started the programme leading to supersonic flight. On the sixth such flight in mid-October 1947 test pilot Yeager lost longitudinal control of the X-1 when flying at Mach 0.94 at 40,000ft. He recovered control and landed on Rogers Dry Lake at Muroc (now Edwards Air Force Base), and both he and the engineers thought that was the end of that road. Magically a solution was provided by Bell almost instantaneously, in the form of a 'field-fix' variation of

the 'flying tail' encountered on the UK visit to Miles Aircraft. Miles had designed their tail arrangement – a single slab tailplane replacing the combined tailplane and elevator – and had flight tested it at slow speed on the Miles Falcon. Bell's control solution was to use the pre-existing tailplane trimmer[1] to modify the incidence of the tailplane in flight, by means of a switch in the cockpit. Whilst not as elegant or user-friendly as a proper 'designed-in' flying tail, it enabled control to be maintained through the critical transonic regime. Two flights after evaluating their ad hoc 'flying tail', on the seventh flight in the USAAF's X-1 supersonic programme, on 14 October 1947, Captain Charles Yeager attained supersonic flight. The date was stage managed to herald the founding of the United States Air Force (USAF) and to mark the demise of the United States Army Air Force (USAAF).

The all-moving tail on the wooden mock-up of the M.52.

1. It is believed that Bell decided to 'beef up' the trimmer system at the design stage, following their visit to Miles, so that it could be used at the high loads that would be encountered at transonic speeds – 'In case the Brits are right!'

The Bell X-1 which was the first aircraft to break the sound barrier and fly at supersonic speed, on 14 October 1947.

Surprisingly a second American visit to Miles Aircraft took place on 8 July 1946 by Major E.H. Hall and Major Kent Parrot of the Air Technical Section of the Military Intelligence Division, that is the Military Attaché's Office. This was arranged by the Ministry of Supply (MoS) and the visitors were given a tour through the plant and observed the jigs, fixtures, parts and mock-up of the M.52. They reported that the first prototype aircraft had been completed and destroyed in a series of static structural tests (presumably at RAE Farnborough), while the second prototype had all jigging and tooling completed and about 90% of all airframe components fabricated, but not assembled. Then comes a statement, 'It is the opinion of this office that the firm may complete the M.52 on its own when the financial atmosphere becomes more propitious. It could be

finished within a month.' There seems no sound basis for this surmise, especially as the visitors had been advised that a programme of unmanned telemetered flights by a series of small models to be constructed by Vickers would still be performed. If this report was taken seriously in the Pentagon it could still have caused a flutter in the USAF dovecote.

The report comments on all major features of the M.52 but omits to say anything significant about the 'flying tail'. Perhaps, in the light of subsequent events, it was not politic to advertise a British stroke of genius in an American military report.

Static structural testing of an aircraft wing being undertaken at RAE Farnborough.

8 The propulsion unit

Power Jets' Wellington, with the W.2/700 jet engine mounted in the tail for test work.

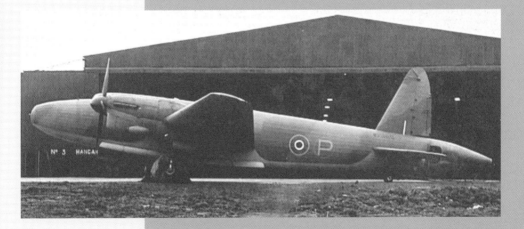

The unit chosen to power the M.52 was the Whittle W.2/700 which was to depend heavily on afterburning to generate the colossal thrust required to punch through the sound barrier. Afterburning, or reheat as it is now often called, is the injection of raw fuel into the jet pipe aft of the turbine. This gives an explosive increase in thrust but also sends fuel consumption rocketing, so is normally only used for specific short-period usages such as take-off, an emergency overtake or evasion manoeuvre in combat, or a supersonic dash.

Whittle's Power Jets company was pioneering this development in flight mainly by installing the W.2/700 in the tail of a Wellington bomber and testing the afterburning in comparative safety till it was deemed reliable enough to go it alone on an actual jet aircraft at RAE. A Meteor 1 was chosen and an aperture was cut out behind the pilot's cockpit so that a flight observer and some test apparatus could be housed in this 'coal hole'. I made the flight with a young observer called Kell, and in general the experiment went very well for a first off. I certainly admired my unseen passenger's nonchalance as he kept reporting results to me. This notable event took place on 1 January 1945, so the New Year literally got off with a bang. However, we were now racing against time, because a potential threat lay in the likely rocketry technology the Allies would inherit from the Germans on the fall of the Third Reich. This could give our competitors in the supersonic pursuit a short cut to success through brute force.

A Meteor 1 at
RAE Farnborough.

In 1944 the W.2/700, which was to power the M.52, was built by Power Jets in limited numbers. The design incorporated reverse-flow combustion chambers and was rated at 2,500lb static thrust, which was to be increased by thrust augmentation. Whittle experimented with a series of thrust augmentors, and No. 4 Augmentor was chosen with the W.2/700 to form a turbo-fan, which in the M.52 had the power further augmented by burning additional fuel after the fan turbine.

This special Whittle engine really consisted of three separate parts, all contained in one 18ft long tube 36 inches in diameter. The first part was a modified W.2/700 engine. Then, secondly, the exhaust from this is passed through the turbine blades of a free-running disc which incorporated compressor blades on its periphery, for a further intake of air. A further set of combustion units added more fuel and heat. Finally the third part was a

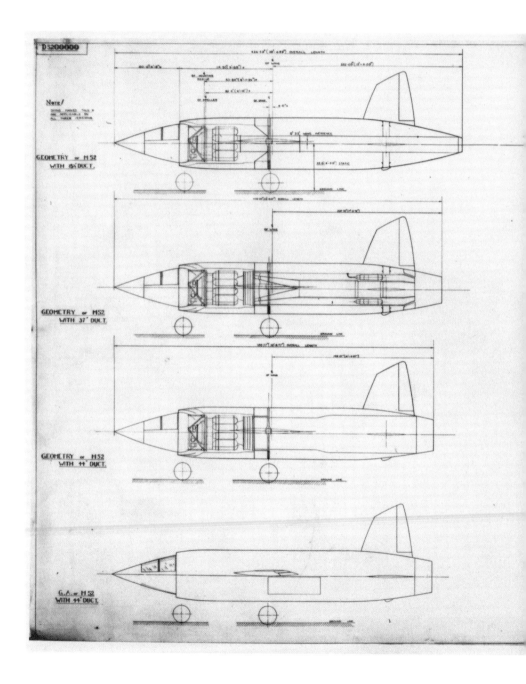

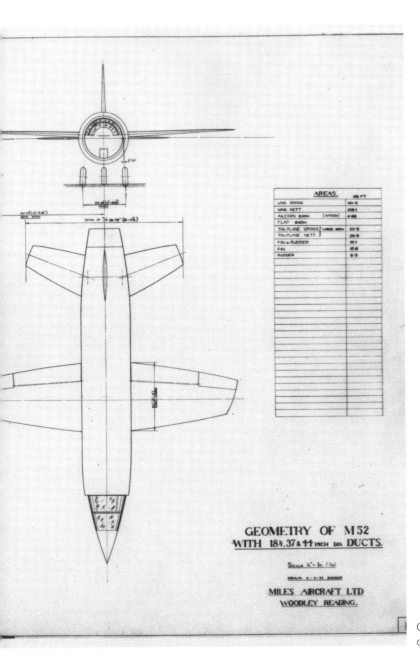

AREAS.	SQ FT
WING GROSS	141·4
WING NETT	108·1
AILERON EACH (APPROX)	4·06
FLAP EACH	
TAILPLANE GROSS / LARGE AREA	53·5
TAILPLANE NETT	36·9
FIN & RUDDER	19·1
FIN	12·6
RUDDER	6·5

GEOMETRY OF M 52
WITH 18½,37&44 INCH DIA DUCTS.

SCALE ½" = 1FT (1/24)

DRAWN 6 - 3 - 55 [illegible]

MILES AIRCRAFT LTD
WOODLEY READING.

General arrangement drawing of Miles M.52.

further air intake that acted as a ram-jet with added burners. The ram-jet effect is of little value at low subsonic speeds, but rapidly becomes of value in the supersonic range. It must be remembered, however, that the intake air must always be slowed to subsonic speeds before entering a compressor.

This engine provided a feature that is also probably unique, and that is while flying at about a Mach number of 1.3 the thrust equals the drag. Beyond that, because of the unique engine, the thrust increases at a greater rate than the drag. This means that if the pilot did not throttle back, the aircraft would accelerate at an ever increasing rate until it self-destructed. In fact the aircraft was designed for a maximum speed of 1,000mph

Mock-up nose of the M.52, showing the annular air intake of the jet engine installation.

at 36,000ft. This speed limit was originally based on the maximum internal engine duct pressure. By simply making this duct stronger and perhaps providing a variable jet nozzle to control the engine over a larger range, this engine limitation to maximum speed could be raised to any desired figure, even to as fast as the heat barrier would permit. However, as the design developed, the temperature of the duct became the critical limiting factor, and this could be adjusted by variation of the jet nozzle.

The installation or housing of the M.52's power plant presented a difficult engineering problem. The fuselage, which was 5ft in diameter, had to provide for the engine which was basically a tube 36 inches in diameter and 18ft long, chiefly containing flaming kerosene under pressure at up to 1,700° absolute (1,427°C), the casing being mainly red hot, and with no structure or control able to run anywhere through or across this engine space. This meant that the fuselage had to be so constructed as to leave a clear 40-inch duct through at least 18ft of it, to allow for the engine and some heat insulation. This left a maximum 10-inch space all round the engine for the structure to take all the wing and tailplane bending moments, controls, fuel tanks, undercarriage, etc. A number of magnesium and light alloy castings were used in this 10-inch space to transfer the loads. The machining of these 5ft diameter items required the acquisition of a large lathe of the type used to manufacture steam locomotive driving wheels.

The engine installation design of the M.52 was criticised for the form of annular air intake, which some 'experts' felt would prove to be less efficient at high speed than a pitot form. This was borne out by experiments later carried out by Power Jets. But the first prototype was not intended to fly supersonically; the second would have been fitted with a variable intake. However, a pitot entry would offer structural advantages, as nose wheel loads would be less concentrated, being distributed through the continuous fuselage skin. The arrangements for jettisoning the cockpit cabin might also prove easier.

While initially hoping that Power Jets could provide full information on their engine at an early stage, it was soon found that this was not available. At the first meeting with Whittle, Miles were informed that there wasn't even a drawing of the complete engine available, and were given a rough sketch of what Power Jets thought it would be like. A preliminary estimate of the weight was provided, as well as the thrust performance, but Miles were told that Power Jets were confident that the developments they were expecting to carry out on the engine would increase the supersonic thrust by about 25% before an aircraft would be ready to take their engine. Miles were also informed that they should provide for a fixed air intake, and Whittle would provide a variable exhaust nozzle to give adequate control of their engine. While Miles were developing the airframe, Power Jets were developing the engine, and a few months later still considered a fixed annular air intake to be satisfactory, but had changed their ideas and considered that the variable exhaust nozzle was no longer necessary. Power Jets continued developing the engine with new materials and ideas, and the results of extensive development testing which they were carrying out.

By early 1945, their engine developments to provide the maximum thrust for the M.52 had led them into a situation where they required different amounts of air into different parts of the engine for different air speeds and flying conditions. However, the first prototype flying aeroplane, using the basic W.2/700 engine, would still only require the fixed annular air intake. But for the second prototype, the supersonic aircraft, all the complicated variations would be needed. All this complication of the various air requirements was, of course, their responsibility to provide, as parts of the power unit. But they did come to Miles, as it appeared to them that the best overall solution to this problem would, in fact, be a variable rather than a fixed air intake. A considerable amount of development work was therefore undertaken, chiefly by Power Jets, to devise the most efficient overall air intake system.

While Miles Aircraft obviously wanted to provide the simplest satisfactory air intake for the engine, the technically best solution had to be a compromise between the complexity of the engine requirements of the air intake and the simplicity of the airframe intake. This resulted in a somewhat complicated system of chambers and moveable flaps as part of the engine installation, as well as the airframe intake also incorporating various flaps, etc., operated by small hydraulic cylinders.

By the time of the cancellation, a working mock-up of at least the Miles variable intake was available, but unfortunately absolutely no drawings or photographs, or even sketches, of any of this later air intake design have been discovered. It may well be that drawings or photographs of this might be in the Power Jets Archives, as they may have survived the obliteration better than the Miles material did.

It was understood that the thrust that Power Jets were estimating for the second flying aircraft's engine at this stage was that which would be given by the air intake they were providing.

It was considered that a minimum of some 200 gallons of fuel would be needed for the high-speed flight. After great difficulty, a scheme was developed comprising five tanks of varying capacities. It was finally found that a total of 250 gallons could be accommodated within the overall 5ft diameter of the fuselage. No extra drop-tank was allowed for, as an extra 50-gallon tank was already designed into the fuselage in case it was required, in addition to the four tanks already in the fuselage holding the normal, specified, 200 gallons. It was unlikely to have been really required because of the fantastically high rate of climb.

It is interesting to compare the Whittle M.52 engine with the much later J-58 engines that powered the SR-71 Blackbird. Both incorporated turbofans to increase mass flow and hence thrust (in the M.52 engine, Whittle's two-stage aft fan, with hot inner and cold outer blades, in the bypass duct). Both incorporated reheat, and both included bypass ducting (see photograph on page 76) to enable the engines to operate effectively as ram-jets

in supersonic flight. Both involved the use of inlet cones. In the case of the M.52, the pilot capsule; in the SR-71, the moveable entry cone (Whittle was already working on variable inlet and exhaust geometry for the M.52 engine). Given that the M.52 engine was conceived in 1943, this is little short of astonishing.

Moreover, it seems likely that, once the aircraft was flying, the ability to cause the nose shock wave to fall just inside the lip of the intake by judicious positioning or adjustment (as on, e.g., the Lightning and other designs using centre-body intake geometry) would doubtless have occurred to the teams involved, and would have aided compression of the ingested air.

The Blackbird SR-71's J-58 engine, showing the horizontal bypass tubes, ducting air from the intake area to the reheat section of the engine.

The Churchill Directive

Ben Lockspeiser's reply to the Churchill Directive.

SECRET

D.S.R. Experimental Aircraft

The following is a brief description of the constructional work which is in hand for research purposes.

Miles E24/43

This aircraft is being built to investigate the problems of flight at speeds exceeding that of sound. The wing section is appropriate to supersonic flight, having sharp leading and trailing edges, and although the machine will not exceed the speed of sound in level flight, it is hoped that it will be possible to do so by diving. The aircraft is a single seater, weighing about 8,000 lb. and is powered by a jet turbine engine, from which additional power is obtained by burning fuel in the jet pipe. The contract SB.27157/C23c was placed on 29.12.43 and the aircraft is expected to be in flight early in 1946.

General Aircraft Tailless Gliders

As part of the research programme on tailless aircraft, General Aircraft are building a number of small gliders to investigate full scale the effect of the various variables of plan form, sweep-back, etc. 6 sets of wings of two different plan forms, and 3 angles of sweep-back are being constructed. Two glider fuselages are being built for these wings and in order to speed up the flight work, two further fuselages with a small power unit will follow on. It is hoped that by the use of power the limitations of glider flight may be relieved. The aircraft accommodate pilot, observer and complete instrumentation, and weigh from 4 to 6,000 lb. The first glider has made one preliminary flight during which some trouble was experienced, but it will be in flight again shortly. The other wings and 2 glider fuselages at regular intervals and the 6 glider wings and 2 glider fuselages at should be completed by the end of the year. The power fuselages at the present rate of progress should be produced early in 1946. Contract No. A/C.3303/C.20(a) was placed 16.9.43.

Armstrong Whitworth E9/44

To extend the scale of the tests an order has been placed with Armstrong Whitworth for a powered tailless aircraft weighing about 30,000 lb. As is well known the tailless aircraft can only compete on level terms with conventional machines when the weight is of the order of 2,000,000 lb. This aircraft can therefore use a representative of one considerably larger. The weight being devoted to the larger ....
scale model of one considerably larger .....
is being devoted to the larger .....
wings. It ...

In early 1945 Prime Minister Churchill issued a Directive (see Appendix 6) to stop all possible research and development work which would not be operational by mid-1946. Where did the M.52 stand in the light of that ultimatum?

By the summer of 1944 the general overall layout of the M.52 had been fixed, and was in fact very similar to the original design submitted to Norbert Rowe of the Directorate of Technical Development (DTD) (see Appendix 2). The relevant drawing was completed on 6 September 1944 (see pages 70–71). Prior to that the Miles Gillette Falcon had been flown on 11 August 1944, and according to the Miles test pilots had shown satisfactory low-speed performance of the bi-convex thin wing. Good lateral control was achieved, with good stalling characteristics and satisfactory longitudinal control with the standard tailplane and elevator.

In April 1945 the fully modified Falcon was flown to RAE and was tested by three RAE High-Speed Flight pilots, including myself. Their reports showed that the aircraft had to be allowed to fly itself off and not pulled off on the take-off run otherwise it would sink back on to the ground. The use of 20° of flap helped in this situation. In the climb 10° of flap improved the rate of climb. The straight stall was innocuous; a dynamic stall gave a sharp wing drop but with no tendency to spin. The aircraft was generally unpleasant to fly in bumpy weather due to lack of trimmers being fitted and lag in elevator effect. Landing presented no problem using 30° of flap and motoring the aircraft right down on to the ground, otherwise a glide hold off got ground effect reactions.

OPPOSITE:
The Churchill Directive.

Copy No.24.

SECRET
W.P.(45) 29
15th January, 1945.
                    WAR CABINET

          Priorities for Research and Development.

               Note by the Prime Minister.

               At the present stage of the war research and
development projects likely to be effectively used in
operations before the end of 1946 must have the highest
priority.

               Research workers and draughtsmen are scanty and
are needed also by industry in preparation for the change-over
to peace-time production and for the development of civil air
transport.

               All Service research and development projects
now in hand must, therefore, be reviewed forthwith in the
light of current hypotheses about the end of the German War
and the duration of the Japanese War. Those which are not
likely to be used in operations on a considerable scale in
the second half of 1946 should be slowed down or temporarily
abandoned so as to permit the maximum concentration upon the
remainder and some release of man-power to civilian production.

               Departments must also review their present
practice in making modifications, particularly to obsolescent
weapons and equipment (including aircraft), so as to cut
out all but those which are essential for operational
purposes or to save life. This replaces my directive of the
16th February, 1943. W.P. (43)54.
                                        W.S.C.

10 Downing Street, S.W.1.
          15th January, 1945.

Ron Smelt, of RAE, whose wind-tunnel-based drag calculations proved to be wildly inaccurate.

Austyn Mair later became Head of the Aeronautical Engineering Department of Cambridge University.

These were low speed tests, but the 'flying tail' (all-moving tailplane) was of course mainly expected to produce great improvements in control at transonic speeds.

To sum up, the M.52 was not going to be an easy aeroplane to fly, but an experienced test pilot should be able to cope with it and achieve the flight parameters to which the aircraft was designed. It should be remembered that the Gillette Falcon was neither fitted with trimmers nor with powered controls, so allowance had to be made for those shortcomings. However, the M.52 was to have had plain flaps, which would have materially improved some of the low-speed characteristics due to the better lift/drag ratio of the plain flap, whereas the Falcon had split flaps.

Perhaps the most discouraging aspects of the M.52 saga were the persistent low performance estimates and pessimistic drag figures issued by Ron Smelt of the RAE, who relied heavily on wind tunnel findings, although the RAE did not have a super-sonic wind tunnel. Fortunately a fresh approach to drag rises in the transonic/supersonic region was provided by RAE's Austyn Mair who relied for his findings on the actual full-scale flight test results from Spitfire and Meteor transonic dives as pub-lished in his classic Report No. Aero 2152. Professor Mair later became Head of the Aeronautical Engineering Department of Cambridge University.

The engine thrusts used by Smelt were out of date, and did not seem to have allowed for the improved turbine material which had been successfully used by Power Jets, or the increased temperatures. Smelt was using a thrust of 4,000lb at 1,000mph compared to the 5,900lb thrust which Power Jets' tests were showing as reasonable at that speed, i.e. 47% greater thrust was available, and the Miles estimate of the drag was 60% less than Smelt's 'guesstimate'.

Based on Mair's more practical approach it was felt that the M.52 was likely to achieve 1,000mph in level flight, but it might be necessary to use a shallow dive to get through the transonic speed region.

Since the late summer of 1944, when the final overall design of the M.52 had been reached, work had been concentrated on the complex detailed design, which demanded unique solutions:

The wing covering: at the time, wings were generally covered with 20 to 22 S.W.G. (0.91 to 0.71mm) Duralumin sheeting, but the very thin wing – 7½% at the root and 4% at the tip – and the very high speed required 10 S.W.G. (3.25mm) plat-ing, and it would have been very difficult to give this a satis-factory three-dimensional double curvature. A simple answer was found by using a single plate of material for each wing surface, and using ribs that just permitted the sheet to bend in one direction and maintain a true cylinder shape, the upper and lower surfaces interconnecting to form the plan form of the leading and trailing edges. The actual wing plan form was, therefore, automatically formed from the selection of the root and tip chords and their thickness chord ratio. This also made model construction out of solid steel much easier.

When designing the M.52's actual wing, it was found that to design a split flap to take the unusually high speeds it would encounter – the best climbing speed was about 600mph – was a disadvantage. A normal flap would be provided at less weight and drag, and this would help both take-off and landing; a plain flap was therefore fitted to the M.52.

A ground test rig was made to develop and test the hydraulic tailplane control, which would give the pilot very considerable power to move the tailplane in supersonic flight, and provide a reserve of power to enable the pilot to control the aircraft in the event of an engine failure at high speed, while reducing speed. The system also provided full manual control at this lower speed, to land safely with no hydraulic power. A fully complex engineering design feat!

A booster jack was built for the hydraulic power boosting of the control surfaces, for power boosted controls were in their infancy in aviation and much had to be learned of their operating characteristics. It was also in turn essential to build a test rig for the booster jack itself.

When the Churchill Directive landed on DSR's desk, Ben Lockspeiser was well aware of the status of the M.52 in its progress towards the first flight. Indeed in the minutes of the 22nd meeting of the Supersonic Committee on 13 March 1945 he said he preferred to see a piloted aircraft for supersonic research, as experience must be gained of flying at the speeds under consideration. Ben Lockspeiser responded to Churchill's Directive with a list of items which he deemed should be exempt from that Directive and therefore should be proceeded with in the country's interest, and the very top item on that list was the M.52 to Specification E.24/43.

10 Barnes Wallis – *éminence grise*

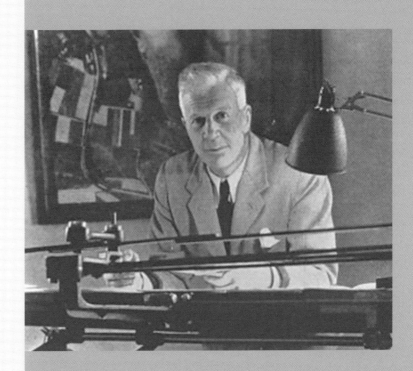

Barnes Wallis at his desk in 1943.

In June 1945 the distinguished but temperamentally unpredictable aviation engineer Barnes Wallis joined the Supersonic Committee, presumably at the invitation of Ben Lockspeiser, a close friend. Barnes Wallis was the designer of the R100 airship, the inventor of geodetic construction, of the bouncing bomb weapon of Dambuster fame, and of variable geometry aircraft.

Since the Dambuster Raid of 1943, Barnes Wallis had been emotionally affected by the number of casualties suffered in that operation and had declared he would seek never to send any young airman to his death if he could possibly avoid it. This could do much to explain his attitude to what he considered the high risk M.52.

The Barnes Wallis philosophy seems to have had its influence on Lockspeiser, for simultaneously with his appointment to the Supersonic Committee, Wallis was asked by Ben Lockspeiser to look into rocket-powered scale model aircraft. By the following meeting, on 10 July 1945, Barnes Wallis had managed to get a contract for 24 rocket-powered models of which the first six were to be of the E.24/43. It is just possible that Lockspeiser originally saw this rocket model route as a cheaper way to supersonic research success in the face of possible escalating costs of the M.52. If so he was going to be severely disillusioned as the eventual model contract cost £400,000 to £500,000. The contract was with Vickers, with whom Barnes Wallis had a long association and was then their Assistant Chief Designer, Aviation Section. It was to develop and produce a number of rocket-driven drop models, the first of which were to be roughly one-third scale models of the M.52 to get transonic and supersonic data.

Although it was known in Britain that Germany was quite heavily involved in wartime rocket technology with the Messerschmitt 163 rocket interceptor fighter and the A4 or V2 rocket missile, the really valuable data on hydrogen peroxide rocket motors was not available till the end of World War II. At first sight it appeared to offer a fast track to supersonic flight, and it certainly caused a hiatus while the newly revealed propulsion possibilities were assessed. Barnes Wallis was not slow to seize on the changed situation, which not only suited his purposes but also sowed doubts in the minds of some proponents of jet propulsion for the M.52.

At the beginning of 1945 even Ronald Smelt suggested that a piloted aircraft should be built around the Me 163 rocket motor, but the strong personality of Barnes Wallis prevailed in the Supersonic Committee, and the models argument won the day.

The legendary rocket-powered Me 163B.

The rocket motor for the Me 163B.

Meanwhile, the Americans were developing their own method of getting into the supersonic race. At an interview some years ago, De Elroy Beeler, who was a Project Engineer at Bell Aircraft and a member of the National Advisory Committee (1941–1958), explained that when Bell was first approached, a jet engine was considered as having a much better fuel consumption – and rockets did explode! Soon, however, it was found that United States knowledge of how to produce a jet engine of sufficient thrust was just not available within a reasonable time scale, but a rocket with sufficient thrust, based on the German designed rockets, would be available much sooner.

The rocket solution was therefore chosen, not by preference but by necessity. The initial US requirement of 1944 was for an aircraft to take off and climb to a height of at least 35,000ft, and then fly level for two to five minutes at 800mph, carrying 500lb of recording instrumentation. But it was soon found that the weight of rocket-fuel for take-off and climb was prohibitive, and a drop launch from a high-flying aircraft would be essential. A normal take-off and landing rocket-driven supersonic aircraft was years away.

The British were streets ahead of the Americans, in that Whittle had produced a unique design for a jet engine that precisely fitted the requirements of an experimental supersonic aircraft. Everyone else could only provide sufficient thrust with a rocket, and try to overcome the extra problems which that would produce. A fuel load of 1,400lb in the M.52 would give power for about 20 minutes' flight, while the same weight of rocket-fuel at that time would only give 25 seconds for the same maximum thrust of 6,000lb. Thus, the Whittle jet engine gave the same supersonic thrust with vastly greater – 60 times – the endurance.

This enabled Miles to produce an aeroplane capable of taking off, climbing, flying level at 1,000mph and landing under its own power, while the enforced rocket choice of the Americans only gave them a dropped manned unit with a rocket booster. Many design problems were therefore different.

While the Americans had the problem of an enormous fuel consumption, at least the rocket motor was relatively small, and the structure could be designed efficiently.

The British had the problem of housing an enormous, red-hot engine in a very small aircraft.

It was suggested in the press in late 1946 that Miles were considering a rocket-powered M.52, dropped from a Lancaster. Little consideration of such a proposal was made at Miles, as no practical advantage was found, and in any case the contract specified an aircraft with the Whittle engine and all aspects of the design were specific to this.

If, for some reason, someone wanted a rocket-driven device, a very different structural design would have been made, although the aerodynamics would probably have been similar. Obviously, a full-span wing spar through the fuselage would have saved weight, and a very much smaller cross-section fuselage would have been chosen – and so on. Really, a very different project would have been necessary. Apart from anything else, a manned, air-launched machine of this nature could not have been tested in Britain, as we simply do not have the Americans' large, flat open spaces and very long runways, which are essential for safe landings of high wing-loaded gliders. Where would

the flight tests have been carried out? But really – why such a change to a much less useful machine when the better aircraft was nearly complete and, if not cancelled (in March 1946), would have flown in three to four months' time?

The British aviation fraternity is firmly convinced that the Bell X-1 owed its success to what the Americans gleaned from

The Bell X-2 which incorporated several of the M.52 design features: a bi-convex wing, an all-moving forty-degree swept tailplane and the pilot escape pod.

their visit to the Miles factory in Autumn 1944, and in particular what Bell learned from the M.52's 'flying tail'. Certainly, in spite of American protestations that they had their own original ideas on a 'flying tail', there does not appear to be any solid evidence of its appearance on test before the X-1 ran into transonic trouble in 1947.

What lends credence to the British viewpoint is Bell's follow-on project after the X-1, a 40-degree swept-wing rocket-powered supersonic research aircraft, constructed of heat resistant alloys, plus a bi-convex wing aerofoil section with a sharp leading edge, an all-moving 40-degree swept tailplane, and a forward cockpit designed as a pilot escape pod. Surely the X-2 did not have these Miles features purely by coincidence.

It is worth recording that I met Barnes Wallis briefly in October 1944 at Beccles airfield where I was involved in the preparations for Operation *High Ball*, a variation on the Dambuster Raid, to be made from aircraft carriers against Japanese capital ships in harbour.

I found him an austere personality, who was unlikely to suffer fools gladly, and who was forceful in his views – and somewhat intolerant of those who questioned those views.

11 The model concept gains ground

A Vickers rocket-propelled
test model of the M.52.

In fairness to Barnes Wallis it has to be said that the possible use of rocket models had already been mooted in the Supersonic Committee meeting on 10 April 1945. This was almost inevitable in the light of what was being revealed of German rocket technology as World War II drew to its close in Europe.

After some discussion it was agreed that both the jet-propelled and rocket-propelled aircraft should be proceeded with. The Chairman was of the opinion that the proposed rocket aircraft should be piloted, and when I got to hear of this it had a decided influence on my already growing motivation to fly the Me 163 under power if possible.

There were those on the Committee who considered that such an aircraft should be radio-controlled for safety considerations. But Ronald Smelt pointed out that it was impossible to investigate the control characteristics without a pilot, and this was necessary in the transition period near Mach 1.0. If an automatic pilot was used the problem would be complicated by stability. Ronald Smelt suggested that scale models be used for investigation of the transition period as far as was possible, with a full-scale aircraft with a pilot to be flown later. This suggestion met with general approval in the Committee, and the Chairman said he would approach Barnes Wallis, who could probably be of assistance in the design of the models.

If Miles had been represented on the Supersonic Committee the April 1945 meeting would undoubtedly have set alarm bells ringing, for other cracks were beginning to appear in the framework of the E.24/43 specification.

From left:
Flight Lieutenant Hugh
V. Kennedy, assistant
test pilot; Tommy Rose,
chief test pilot, who
retired in January 1946;
George Miles and Don
Brown – all Ministry
approved test pilots.
Only Hugh Kennedy
was small enough to fly
the M.52; all lacked jet
and transonic testing
experience.

To my mind the biggest mistake made was to hand over the complete M.52 data to the Americans in autumn 1944. There was no obvious war-related urgency to offer such co-operation as Britain had done earlier with its invention of the jet engine. We had a substantial time lead over any other aviation country in the race to the prestigious goal of supersonic flight and we gifted it away. Perhaps there was some overriding political reason for this philanthropic gesture, but if so it has not surfaced to date.

Aero Flight at RAE had a little worry of its own about the sanguine handling reports of flight tests carried out on the Gillette Falcon by Miles pilots and which seemed to skirt round some of the issues that we felt were vital to investigate. We were not overly concerned because we well knew that company test pilots had a tendency to be optimistic in reporting on their firms' products, and we would later have our own chance to fly the Gillette Falcon and make our own independent assessments.

The three highly experienced pilots of RAE's High-Speed Flight made their flight tests on the Gillette Falcon at Farnborough. All came to much the same conclusion – that the aircraft was not particularly pleasant to fly, but its shortcomings were not sufficient to preclude it from achieving its intended specialist task. However, the CO of the High-Speed Flight was Squadron Leader Tony Martindale, who made the famed dive in a Spitfire XI to Mach 0.92 on 27 April 1944. He concluded his report on the Gillette Falcon with the damning words: 'It appears to me the step from this to the supersonic aeroplane is a very large one and might easily land the first pilot to fly the latter in considerable trouble.' Martindale's reputation was such that those words were unlikely to fall on deaf ears in the upper echelons of the Ministry of Aircraft Production.

Another unpredictable factor that cast its influence over aviation worldwide was the effect of the wealth of advanced aeronautical technology that became available on the demise of the Third Reich. In the area of high-speed performance not only was the potential of rocketry revealed, but also the plethora of

The ill-fated de Havilland 108 transonic research aircraft.

new aerodynamic shapes that resulted from extensive tests in the German supersonic wind tunnels. Information on wing sweepback and forward sweep, all-wing and delta wing shapes cascaded into the aviation world and virtually stopped it in its tracks. Aircraft designers paused to assess this sudden gold rush of aerodynamic data, and some rushed to utilise it, with varied success as in the case of the de Havilland 108 and the Northrop YB-49 bomber.

There is no doubt that this flood of revolutionary technology impacted on the Supersonic Committee, where discussions on

The revolutionary Northrop YB-49 all-wing bomber.

rocketry and the effects of wing sweepback were particularly rife, and tended to destabilise progress on the M.52 by sowing doubts in the minds of those that controlled its fate.

Yet another factor that was unsettling for M.52 protagonists was the sudden flurry of practical experimentation in ejection seat technology by the Martin-Baker company. Again this was a field in which German engineers had significant success. The M.52's pilot safety capsule had suffered criticism from a number of quarters as being its Achilles heel. Indeed the decision had been made not to incorporate it in the first prototype aircraft, but to wait until it was further developed for incorporation in the second prototype intended to undertake the supersonic flights. I must emphasise, however, that I had always expressed my confidence in the capsule arrangement.

And so we arrived at the summer of 1945 in an atmosphere of slight ambivalence surrounding the future of the M.52 as far as the Supersonic Committee was concerned. But there was nothing but solid support for the project from the Miles team, Morien Morgan's RAE Aero Flight Section team, and from Power Jets.

It was learnt after the fall of Germany that a cockpit escape capsule of similar design to that of the M.52 had been fitted in the He 176, the liquid rocket-powered aircraft which made its first historic flight on 20 June 1939.

12 The Power Jets crisis

Frank Whittle with a model of his W.2/700 engine.

All was not gloom and doom for the M.52 in the latter half of 1945, for on 13 November final agreement was reached with the MAP that arrangements for pilots' safety were satisfactory. Also by December Power Jets had developed the W.2/700 engine to give a thrust of 6,950lb at 1,000mph at 36,000ft on a cold day with an air temperature of 10°C below ICAN.

Power Jets had been started in 1936 by Frank Whittle and some close working colleagues to develop and build jet engines, and eventually by 1943 had a workforce numbering 600. It had always been run on a financial shoestring and in order to improve this situation Frank proposed to the Government that it be nationalised, together with other companies engaged on similar technological work. In the event this proposal rebounded badly on Whittle and his was the only such enterprise nationalised on 28 April 1944, with Dr Roxbee Cox, Director of Special Projects at MAP, appointed as Chairman and Managing Director; Whittle later became Technical Adviser to the Board. The appointment of Roxbee Cox was good news as he was a powerful supporter of the gas turbine and a member of the Supersonic Committee, and he hit it off with Whittle's somewhat difficult personality.

The crux of the crisis that built up in Power Jets was that Frank Whittle was strongly of the opinion that the company should design and produce gas turbines, as promised when the firm was nationalised.[1] The private manufacturers, however, were adamant that, to avoid unfair competition, Power Jets should be restricted to research and development only, and that all design, development and production of actual jet engines must be left to the big boys like Rolls-Royce and de Havilland. Whittle's stance on this

1. A letter from the Minister of Aircraft Production to Power Jets (R & D) Ltd, dated 27 April 1944, contained a list of the primary objectives which he wished the board to carry out. This included: (2) To design, construct and develop prototype engines, components and accessories ... and (3) To manufacture small batches of such engines ...

Dr Roxbee Cox (later Lord Kings-Norton), Director of Special Projects at MAP.

issue was immoveable and on 22 January 1946 he sent Roxbee Cox his letter of resignation, and followed this up on 24 January with a similar letter to Air Marshal Sir Alec Coryton, Controller of Research and Development at MAP.

This action by Whittle led to the inevitable break up of his original pioneer team, sixteen key members of which resigned en bloc. Power Jets remained in being as a small patent-holding company, while the manufacturing and experimental resources as well as the flight testing unit were taken over by the newly constituted National Gas Turbine Establishment.

There is little doubt that powerful forces – politicians, government officials and industrial moguls – had operated against Power Jets since 1940, all with different motives but with a common aim – to destroy the company.

The attacks on Power Jets were hardly deserved because it was leading the field in manufacturing methods and in gas turbine technology. But it has to be admitted that Rolls-Royce was catching up fast and had greater knowledge of production methods.

In the course of these shenanigans Whittle remained dedicated to the M.52, but it was inevitable that progress in developing the W.2/700 engine suffered with so many distractions, and this in turn increased costs. However, it must be emphasised that up to the end of 1945 there was no slow-up on the engine that would have justified drastic ministerial interference. The estimated performance of the M.52 with W.2/700, up to July 1944, was:

Max speed without augmentor:	585mph at 30,000ft	Take-off distance to 50ft:	4,560ft (at AUW of 7,710lb)
Max speed with augmentor:	705mph at sea level	Wing loading:	54.5lb/sq ft (at AUW 7,710lb)
Max speed at 36,000ft after dive from 50,000ft:	1,000mph	Main dimensions:	Span: 26ft 10.5in. Length: 33ft 6.22in.
		Aspect ratio:	5.09 gross
Best climbing speed:	600mph	Wing area:	141.4sq ft
		Net wing area:	108.1sq ft

These figures had materially improved by the start of 1946 (see Appendix 8). With the passage of time the general concensus of opinion is that the MoS made the right decision about Power Jets' future role, and that Whittle over-reacted in his disappointment. Certainly his resignation tore the heart out of Power Jets, and caused what must now be judged as irreparable damage to the M.52.

At this stage in the M.52's history the prototype build was 90% complete towards the first flight, aimed for in the first quarter of 1946. Understandably the Miles and RAE Aero teams were alight with anticipation, although outwardly there were no obvious signs of the inward excitement because of the tight security surrounding the project.

I had now been firmly told by Morien Morgan that I would be making the first flight of the M.52 from Boscombe Down, so I was mentally getting myself geared up for the task. Since first being advised that I was to be part of the M.52 team I had had the opportunity to substantially increase my flight testing experience, particularly in the transonic range, largely due to the acquisition of the examples of advanced German aircraft that were captured at the end of World War II.

Although there was some dismay at Frank Whittle's departure from Power Jets, there was no panic that a cataclysmic disaster had befallen the M.52 project. Perhaps the aura of unreality that surrounded the awesome prospect of breaking the sound barrier had lulled us into thinking that our only danger of disaster would be at high speed in the air – and not in the boardrooms of the Ministry of Supply and Aircraft Production.

This period was the lull before the storm for the M.52, and to me it is quite inexplicable that no real hint of the impending crash filtered through to the Miles and RAE teams, who were in upbeat mood when lightning struck.

13 The final blow

Among the prominent
reasons mooted for
cancellation of the M.52
was pilot safety.
But this final approved
version of the pilot
escape capsule was
accepted by the
Ministry of Supply and
Aircraft Production.

There can be no doubt that Frank Whittle's resignation from Power Jets ruffled a good few feathers in the Ministry of Supply and indeed in the Government itself. In some quarters there was positive outrage that he should cock a snook at the Establishment in that way.

Although there must have been some unrecorded discussions at the Ministry, the official move to cancel the M.52 took place at the 31st meeting of the Supersonic Flight Committee, held on 12 February 1946. It was stated at this meeting that 'the opinion of the Committee was unanimous that there was no case for continuing on the grounds of obtaining information at transonic or supersonic speeds (the reason for placing the contract). A case was, however, put forward for the completion of the aircraft for use as a test bed of the engine'.

This statement was, of course, ridiculous, as any full-scale transonic and supersonic information was urgently required and the M.52 would have provided it. Obviously the 17 members present could not really have believed such a statement and even the Ministry must have thought this reason so impossible that they never used it to the public as a reason for cancelling the M.52 contract.

This bombshell was conveyed to Miles Aircraft by letter without any prior form of communication, and this is how we learnt of it in Aero Flight at RAE. I was so incensed that in the evening I called on Sir Ben Lockspeiser, who lived just round the corner from me at Farnborough. He knew me and agreed to see me, but it was a waste of time for he said the matter was highly classified and not up for discussion, and that it may turn out to be better for me in the long term. I did not understand that remark, because if he was referring to my pilot safety, his Supersonic Committee had at their 29th meeting on 13 November 1945 accepted that the proposed escape capsule separation arrangements satisfactorily covered the pilot's safe escape.

Indeed from that point in time the true reason for the cancellation of the M.52 has remained shrouded in mystery. Dennis Bancroft has devoted some fifty years of his life trying to unravel that mystery, and here is what he has to say in what is an abbreviated version of his full report of December 1997.

Supersonic Committee meeting No. 31, 12 February 1946
For some time it has been obvious that the results of what was discussed at the 31st Supersonic Committee meeting really put in train the cancellation of the E.24/43 contract. With this knowledge, some years were spent trying to find a copy of the minutes of this particular meeting without success. The main part of my report was based on the only available written information on what was discussed, as given by Mr Vessey's[1] memo of the day following the meeting, reporting the almost unbelievable fact that 'the opinion of the Committee was unanimous that there was no case for continuing on the grounds of obtaining information at transonic or supersonic speeds (the reason for placing the contract). A case was, however, put forward for the completion of the aircraft for use as a test bed of the engine.'

Now the minutes have been found, as a result of some inspired detective work by Josh Spoor, who has devoted years to this project. They give a very different account of what occurred at this meeting from Mr Vessey's statement. In fact, the statements recorded in the minutes of this meeting do not even agree with minutes of statements made at earlier meetings. Of course, it may well be that the minutes do not reflect what was actually said at the meeting, but instead are a set of minutes which the meeting may have agreed to have entered, as the true discussion would not be politically wise to write down,

1. Mr Vessey was Assistant Director, Armament Research Dept at the MoS.

as does happen. However, whatever may have been the case, these written minutes must have been acceptable to all the members present, as this part of the minutes was approved without amendment by the following meeting. Incidentally, no mention of the cancellation of this contract was ever made in that or later meetings of this Committee. Therefore, we must consider each of the items actually written in the minutes as being the meeting's genuine opinion, in the absence of evidence to the contrary. We will therefore consider in detail minute 4.3 E.24/43 of the meeting on 12 February 1946:

A. The original estimate of £130,000 for two aircraft and a test fuselage had now been increased to £250,000 all told, and the Contracts Department asked if it was justified to continue the project.

It is well known that it is always very expensive to cancel a contract part-way through, as much of the materials and sub-contracting work, etc., has been committed, and only the direct labour charges in the final assembly can be saved. In this case, the commitments at this time were such that not more than £84,000 could have been saved by cancelling at this stage. Presumably the meeting was not very worried by such small amounts of money, as they had either just awarded, or were at that time putting through, a new contract with Vickers (Barnes Wallis) for rocket-driven dropped models at a cost of some £400,000–£500,000, which even Lockspeiser had earlier stressed could not give the desired information (see his wish for a piloted aircraft, minutes of the 22nd meeting, 13 March 1945).

B. The Chairman summarised his reasons for feeling that the work should stop:

(i) 'The performance would not be as good as had been hoped.' In fact this is not true, and the information available at that time proved that it was almost certain to be somewhat better than was originally specified. The Committee members should have known that, and it is almost unbelievable if they didn't. But it is just conceivable that they could still have been working on the old, uncorrected, RAE figures which gave a wildly pessimistic maximum speed of 630mph. If, however, they honestly believed that the maximum speed would be only 630mph, surely the contract should have been cancelled years earlier, as no useful purpose would have been achieved by continuing. But minute No. 5.1 of the 26th meeting on 14 August 1945 reported on a meeting held on 30 July 1945 at which, presumably, members of Miles Aircraft, including myself, would have been present. It was reported that this meeting had 'cleared all the outstanding problems on E.24/43 save that of pilot's escape' – which must have meant that, among other matters, the performance was agreed to be up to the 1,000mph specification and the pessimistic RAE data had at last been corrected. Therefore, it should have been obvious to the Committee, from their own previous minutes, that performance was no longer a problem.

(ii) 'There was, moreover, apparently insuperable difficulty in assuring the safety of the pilot.' This is an odd statement to make at the 31st meeting, as minute No. 4.2 of the 29th meeting on 13 November 1945 states 'Mr Vessey reported that a recent meeting had decided that the pilot's escape from the E.24/43 could be satisfactorily covered by cabin jettisoning alone' and work had therefore proceeded along those lines.

(iii) 'Servicing problems were also considerable.' Obviously, the servicing of an experimental supersonic aircraft, when so much had to be packed into such small spaces, would be more complicated than normal aircraft of the period. The fastest then available aeroplanes, such as the Spitfire, would have a single panel, held with two or three rapidly detachable clips, to permit the whole panel to hinge out, giving access to a complete side of an engine. This type of servicing was, of course, impossible at this period for a supersonic aircraft, as much tighter fitting of the panel was required, with numerous additional screws to keep it in place. But all supersonic aircraft would be more complex to service than normal subsonic ones. For example, even the Concorde takes about four times as much servicing as a Boeing 747. The M.52, however, did have rapidly openable doors for the various instrumentation cameras, etc., to be accessed, but most of the aircraft was really just a large, tubular engine. I feel that 'servicing problems' would be quite irrelevant to serious considerations of cancellation, and had never been raised before.

(iv) Sir Ben also felt that it would not be justified to go on just to help develop an engine with afterburning.

Conclusions

Though we have now found the minutes of the Supersonic Committee meeting of 12 February 1946, where undoubtedly the ultimate discussion was held which led directly to the cancellation of the M.52, we still do not seem to know what was actually said at the meeting and on what grounds the cancellation was really based. The written minutes only give reasons which the Committee members should have already known to be untrue, and even Mr Vessey, writing the following day, gives a very different interpretation of what was said.

The underlying reason for the cancellation of an aircraft which was known at the time (and substantiated afterwards) to be almost certain to exceed its original specification must still, therefore, be circumstantial. Although I still feel that 'flattening' Whittle – i.e. what the written minutes left unsaid – is the real reason, there is another possibility, though anyone who was not familiar with Ministry workings would think it ludicrous! This is that the seventeen members present at the 31st meeting of the Supersonic Committee came to the decision in good faith to cancel the M.52 and lost for ever Britain's supremacy in supersonic flight. They based their decision on wildly erroneous, pessimistic and out-of-date drag and performance information from the RAE, in spite of the fact that their own recent minutes would appear to indicate that they had received later, more correct data. If they did really believe the early, terrible performance estimates given by the RAE, they ought to have cancelled the project then and there, instead of which it went on for another two years! The question of pilot safety can be discounted, because the Committee had already accepted Miles Aircraft's provision of a jettisoning cockpit to be adequate for this.

Therefore, it was not the lack of performance, it was not the pilot safety and it was not the cost to complete. So what else could it have been? For it not to have been mentioned in the minutes it must have been political – and the most political item on their plate at that moment was the problem of Whittle and the private engine makers, as concluded in my original Report. Hardly a sufficient reason to throw away Britain's future as the supersonic leader of the world, but the finding of the minutes has reinforced my original conclusions, rather than weakened them.

14 Red herrings

- ○ Supersonic body shape
- ○ Wing loading
- ○ Climb performance
- ○ Straight wing versus sweepback
- ○ Political pressures
- ○ Centrifugal versus axial flow jets

In the previous chapter the possible main reasons to cancel the M.52 have been dealt with, but in the long hiatus period of the search to find the truth a variety of possible reasons surfaced. These are now examined further and exposed as red herrings.

1. **Greater research needed to determine the characteristics of the best supersonic body by an extensive model testing programme.** According to *The Aeroplane* of 6 May 1947 this was the reason for the cancellation (see Appendix 7) given to it by Sir Ben Lockspeiser, who envisaged 'as many as 100 models might be necessary, and as the models are being made in sixes, there are likely to be some 18 different shapes. The first batch of six models will bear the same external shape as the M.52 to coordinate the work already done by Miles and elsewhere.'

   Information on body shape is more fully known than any other supersonic problem, as ballistic tests at sub- and supersonic speeds have been undertaken for many years, and new shapes are easily tested. The problems of achieving supersonic flight are not associated with the main body shape.

2. **Possible take-off and wing-loading problems of the M.52 design.** Some views were expressed that the bi-convex wing and the wing loading would have produced an aircraft unsafe for take-off and landing, but the take-off wing loading for the initial flights was 42.7lb/sq ft, reducing to about 39lb/sq ft for landing. For comparison, I had already flown the Seafire 47 at a wing loading of 42.2lb/sq ft.

   The take-off wing loading with the W.2/700 engine and the No. 4 Augmentor for the supersonic flights would be

55.4 lb/sq ft. For comparison I had already flown the German Me 262 at a wing loading of 64lb/sq ft and it had only about half the thrust/weight ratio of the M.52.

The 1944 estimate for the take-off run to a height of 50ft was 1,200 yards for the W.2/700 initial tests, and 1,500 yards with the No. 4 Augmentor because of the latter's weight. However, by 1945 Power Jets had developed and run the engine using the improved Nimonic 90 turbine blades, and raised the engine speed from 16,750rpm to 17,600rpm to give a 25% increase in static thrust. This improved take-off performance significantly.

3. **Possible inadequate climb performance and/or excessive fuel consumption.** It was suggested in an article in *Aerospace* magazine of September 1992 that the drag characteristics of the bi-convex wing and/or the high fuel consumption were such that the specific ceiling of 40,000ft could not be obtained and would thereby prevent supersonic flight.

Actually the drag of a bi-convex wing is higher in climb than an orthodox section. But the enormous power of the engine compensates for this, and a rate of climb of over 15,000ft/min would have been obtained with a ceiling of at least between 50,000 and 60,000ft. These estimated performance figures were confirmed in RAE Tech. Note No. Aero 1470 of July 1944. The 25% increase in engine thrust available by 1945 would improve both rate of climb and ceiling considerably.

Miles Aircraft's estimated drag and Power Jets' calculated thrust showed that from about Mach 1.1 to 1.2 the drag was likely to be a little greater than the thrust available. Therefore a shallow dive to get through this range may have been required, but not on a cold day.

Having achieved about Mach 1.2, however, the excess thrust over drag became greater the faster one flew and the maximum speed would be limited only by the critical engine temperature, the exhaust nozzle size selected having been chosen to achieve the goal of 1,000mph. The proposed flight plan of a typical 1,000mph flight was:

> From an initial rate of climb of 15,000ft/min, level off at 50,000ft and then dive at about 8 degrees to accelerate through the sound barrier to a speed of 1,000mph in under one minute, then fly level for 30 miles at this speed for under two minutes. The pilot would throttle back and climb again to almost 50,000ft to slow down to 500mph, turning slowly through 180 degrees, and glide the 90 miles to base in 10 minutes with sufficient fuel remaining for a power-on landing at about 170mph. Flight duration would be 20 minutes.

4. **The M.52's orthodox wing plan was out of date and a redesigned swept-back wing layout would be better.** Swept wings delay the onset of compressibility effects in seeking to achieve supersonic speed, but they may not necessarily be the most efficient plan form from a drag point of view. A straight wing of very thin aerofoil section may be even more efficient while offering simpler structural advantages. In later years the delta wing proved to be the most efficient supersonic plan form, but it was unproven in the 1940s.

5. **Possible USA Government pressure to cancel.** Although the USA now had full knowledge of the M.52, following the visit of their representatives to Miles Aircraft Ltd in autumn 1944, and must have realised that Great Britain was leading the race to achieve supersonic flight, we have found no evidence to suggest American political pressure to thwart the M.52 from gaining this prestigious milestone prize in aviation history.

6. **Possible RAE request to drop the Whittle centrifugal compressor jet engine in favour of an axial-flow type engine favoured by the National Gas Turbine Establishment (NGTE) at Pyestock.** This suggestion originated from a former Royal Canadian Air Force officer who had served at Pyestock during

1944 and up to June 1945. He had written a number of reports emphasising the fact that axial compressors are more efficient than centrifugal types at higher compression ratios.

Apart from the W.2/700 plus the No. 4 Augmentor there has never been an engine which could approach the Whittle design for this particular job. The M.52 required some 6,000lb thrust at supersonic speeds. Whittle's No. 4 Augmentor achieved this for an added 300lb of engine weight plus some 100lb of large ducting and an extra burner. A ram jet is inefficient at low transonic and even low supersonic speeds, but a considerable increase in thrust at supersonic speed for a weight increase of only 400lb made the whole concept of a supersonic research M.52 a reality.

The possibility has occurred to some that another secret supersonic project may have been mooted and caused a hiatus in the support of the M.52. Well, there was the RAE Transonic Research Aircraft proposed by Professors Multhopp and Winter, two distinguished German aeronautical scientists brought to the RAE by the Farren Mission at the end of World War II. Their project proposal was not published till February 1948, and it was full of innovations (pilot prone position, heavily sweptback wings and tail unit, skid type undercarriage, downward pilot ejections).

This project proposal may not have been available to the Supersonic Committee before the cancellation of the M.52, but its innovatory ideas were being bandied from mid-1945 onward.

However, it was not until 1947 that contracts were placed for (a) three prototype English Electric P.1 research aircraft with swept wings and (b) two Fairey Delta 2 delta-winged research aircraft. It was to be seven years after the contracts were placed before the first flights were made by both these aircraft.

The list of red herrings – or more aptly called smoked herrings – has proved to be of no substance, but has contributed to setting up a smoke screen to further obscure the real motive for the cancellation of the M.52, which still remains a mystery today.

15 Test history of the M.52 rocket models

The English Electric Lightning, developed from the P.1A aircraft, first flew in 1954.

As we have already seen in Chapter 10, Barnes Wallis had, by mid-1945, secured a contract for 24 rocket-powered models. By mid-1947 the first of these models had been completed in the configuration of the M.52, taken aloft under a Mosquito and lost in turbulence before flight. More disasters were to follow, with only the final flight, on 10 October 1948, being successful. It was intended that further models would have different aerodynamic shapes such as swept-back wings, delta plan forms, and tailless variants.

The model rocket-powered M.52 had provision for fuel tanks where the engine used to be, and an auto-pilot in place of the pilot's cockpit. It proved to be no mean task to pack all the required equipment into the slender streamlined body of the model, of which the wing span was only about 8ft. The power plant used was a development of the bifuel rocket used in the German Me 163 and generated some 900lb thrust.

The models were launched from a Mosquito Mk 16 at 36,000ft over the sea off the Isles of Scilly. After dropping 1,000ft to clear its carrier, the model should accelerate and reach its maximum speed in level flight at the end of 70 seconds.

Telemetering equipment in the model relayed to ground receivers such data as height, speed, Mach number, thrust, drag, tailplane angle and the like during the model's acceleration through the sonic range of speeds and during its subsequent deceleration. During its flight the model was to be tracked by radar, which should provide a close check on the telemetered

OPPOSITE:
The M.52 rocket model in flight.

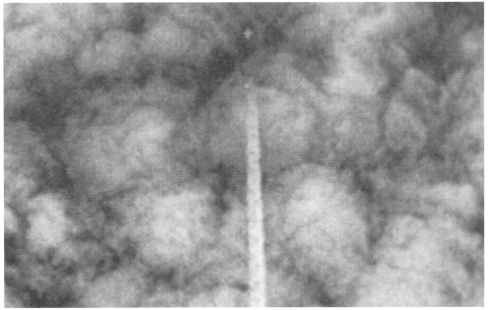

information. In addition a Meteor jet aircraft was to be used for air-to-air photography.

The Mosquito carrying the M.52 model, with its crew before take-off on 8 October 1947.

As, even after the motor stops, the model would have enough speed to fly 150 miles, and might therefore be a danger to shipping, the controls were locked by clockwork to ensure that the model plunged into the sea 15 miles away from the launch.

The first attempt to launch the M.52 model, on 30 May 1947, ended in disaster when the aircraft lost control and the model fell off before it could be launched.

The first launch of the model was made on 8 October 1947 out of St Eval in Cornwall, but was unsuccessful. It appears that the 'Alpha' rocket motor exploded after the fuel metering orifices in the combustion chamber had become iced up. There is a certain irony in this, as if that minor disaster was telling us we should have stuck with the full-scale M.52, as the Americans achieved supersonic flight with the Bell X-1 only six days later, on 14 October 1947. Somehow I could have stomached my disappointment at not being the first pilot to break the sound barrier if our pilotless M.52 had done it, as indeed it later did.

Exactly twelve months later, on 10 October 1948, the last of the Vickers models of the M.52 was launched successfully from a Mosquito at about 400mph at 36,400ft altitude, west of St Mary's in the Isles of Scilly. The rocket fired correctly six seconds after launch and the model accelerated to 934mph, equivalent to Mach 1.38 in level flight, 62 seconds after release. This was the only Vickers model to have achieved a successful mission, but instead of ending it by diving into the sea as planned, it was last observed heading west on auto-pilot 60 miles from the launching position off the coast.

In addition to proving that the M.52 design remained stable throughout the subsonic, transonic and supersonic regimes, the model also enabled supersonic drag coefficients to be evaluated that were fully 20% lower than those the M.52 drag estimates had used. Even allowing for the model's lack of an annular air intake (the model's intake was faired over), this proves that Miles' drag estimates for the full-size M.52 were actually pessimistic to a significant degree, and that its performance would have been even better than had been anticipated.

This most expensive Vickers Model Test Programme, which reputedly cost in excess of £400,000, only achieved one actual successful 50-second powered flight. But this confirmed that the M.52 was a satisfactory design and would almost certainly have reached the 1,000mph design requirement. However, the total cost of the M.52 up to the time of its cancellation, and the additional expenditure to complete it, would only have been about half the cost of the one successful model flight. If nothing else this final model flight confirmed the soundness of the M.52 design, and that it would probably have achieved its goal two years earlier and with a saving of £350,000. The fact that the M.52 would have been reusable and not just a one-third scale throw-away model of the M.52 should not be forgotten.

It is interesting to compare the flight testing of the American Bell X-1 before it made its historic first supersonic flight on 14 October 1947. Bell Aircraft had firstly to complete airworthiness demonstrations of the X-1 aeroplanes, but its location in Buffalo meant that the poor winter weather in that location would lead to long delays, so the whole operation was moved to Florida. The Army Air Field at Pinecastle was selected because it had a 10,000ft runway, suitable for the initial flights of the X-1 as a glider.

The first such flight by Bell test pilot Jack Woolams was made on 25 January 1946, followed by a few similar flights, which unexpectedly encountered weather problems. So the decision was made to move to Muroc USAAF Base in California's Mojave Desert, which had the adjacent Rogers Dry Lake, offering some 14 miles of usable landing surface.

Glide flight testing by Bell recommenced on 10 April 1947, by which time a radar tracking station and 13 support personnel for the X-1 had been set up at Muroc. By 5 June 1947 Bell had completed its flight demonstration programme with a total of nine glide flights on the No. 1 aeroplane, which was then handed over to the USAAF. The USAAF conducted its first glide flight on 6 August 1947, flown by Captain Yeager, who then carried out 23 flights between August 1947 and April 1948.

In parallel with the USAAF flights, the NACA Muroc Flight Test Unit conducted its own tests on the No. 2 aeroplane, after Bell test pilot Chalmers Goodlin made the first rocket flight on 9 December 1946, and on 17 January 1947 reached a Mach number of 0.82. Bell concluded its flight demonstration on that aeroplane by 29 May 1947, and Yeager flew the acceptance flight for NACA on 25 September 1947.

16 The aftermath

The Cathedral, a specially
equipped building at
RAE Farnborough, for
static structural
destruction tests.

The immediate effect of the M.52 cancellation on those closely associated with the project was downright disbelief. When the dreadful realisation dawned on us that it was hard fact, there was a period of stunned incredulity, while each participant assessed in his mind how he personally would be affected and how the country's prestige would suffer from this devastating blow, and was there any way to recover from it.

In my own case I was on a high at the time, for I had just made the world's first aircraft carrier landing of a jet aircraft on 3 December 1945, some seven months ahead of the Americans. I was also poised to break the sound barrier about October 1946, which as it turned out would have been a year ahead of the Americans. The M.52 cancellation was therefore a particularly bitter blow for me.

The main sufferers of course were the Miles Aircraft personnel, who had dedicated themselves to the M.52 in the belief that it would give Great Britain the kind of prestige that Concorde was to bring in 1960. Although some may have felt that the Miles company could have completed the build of the M.52 as a private venture, this was a pipe-dream. The sad truth was it was the beginning of the end for Miles Aircraft as a manufacturer.

With the cancellation came a directive from the MoS that they would remove all the hardware, drawings, photographs, reports, etc. so far produced by Miles in connection with the M.52 project within a month (March 1946). It has been rumoured that specific instruction was received to dispatch the completed first prototype to RAE Farnborough for static structural destruction tests in the Cathedral, a specially equipped building at RAE for such purposes. Although it is assumed that the tests of the M.52 took place, no confirmation of this has been found.

In normal circumstances a third aircraft, in addition to the two flight prototypes, was to have been prepared specially for structural destruction tests, but does not appear to have had work started on it. The second prototype had all jigging and tooling completed and about 90% of all airframe components fabricated but not assembled. It is believed possible that this second prototype finished up on the scrap dump at Woodley.

News of the cancellation of the M.52 was not made public till September 1946 and features on the research aircraft were published in *Flight* and the *Aeroplane* aviation magazines in the middle of that month. However, the popular media coverage was widespread and overwhelmingly expressed outrage at the perfunctory manner of the cancellation and the resultant loss of prestige in keeping Britain's name in the forefront of world aviation. The *Daily Express* was particularly vehement in seeking public support to reinstate the M.52, but the die had been irrevocably cast with political cunning and chicanery.

The real end effect of all this was not only to give the Americans a clear field to take the winning riband in the supersonic stakes. It left us trailing out of sight for seven years till the English Electric P.1A research aircraft and the Fairey Delta 2 research aircraft both first flew in 1954.

In February 1955 the Conservative Government published a White Paper 'The Supply of Military Aircraft' in which it was stated that the cancellation of the M.52 'seriously delayed the progress of aeronautical research in the UK' (see Appendix 9).

In October 1955 the Fairey Delta 2 made its first supersonic flight, and on 10 March 1956 it achieved a world record of 1,132mph (Mach 1.73), 30% greater than the American-held record. It is perhaps delayed justice that the pilot Peter Twiss and I were on the same Fleet Air Arm flying course in December 1939.

The English Electric Lightning, developed from the P.1A research aircraft of 1947.

At the end of World War II, when I had the opportunity to make an extensive assessment of Germany's advance aviation technology, I would certainly have placed that country as the front runner in the race to break the sound barrier. The aircraft manufacturers in the Third Reich were bursting with exotic designs for high performance military aircraft, but the only establishment working on a supersonic research aircraft was the German Research Institute for Gliding (DFS) with centres at Darmstadt, Ainring and Hörsching.

This project was being undertaken at Ainring on the DFS 346, with work starting on 1 August 1944 on what was to be a

The tailless Fairey Delta 2, the first aircraft to exceed 1,000mph in level flight. It was piloted by Peter Twiss.

very innovative aircraft. By November 1944 the decision was made, largely as a result of DFS's extensive tests on the Me 163, to go for rocket power as most likely to give a chance to attain supersonic flight. By the end of that month a contract was given to the Siebel firm to formulate the design and construction of the 346. The Siebel company in Halle, Berlin, had roughly the same standing in the German aircraft manufacturers' league as did Miles Aircraft in Britain.

Two different versions of the 346 were to be built, one with a single rocket and the other with two rockets mounted one on top of the other. The wings were to have 45 degrees of sweepback, and the pilot was to be in the prone position, as with the DFS 228 experimental glider. A landing skid was to be used and the aircraft air-launched from a bomber.

Towards the end of the war the Siebel works at Halle were overrun by Russian troops, who found the design drawings and part construction of the 346, which was planned to be completed by the summer of 1945. Realising the potential of their find,

The single rocket
version of the DFS 346.

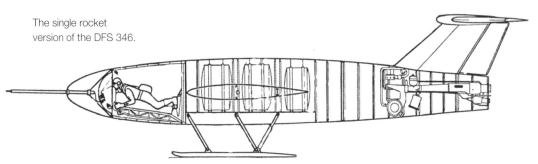

A damaged DFS 228 V1,
recovered from Germany
and taken to RAE
Farnborough in 1945.

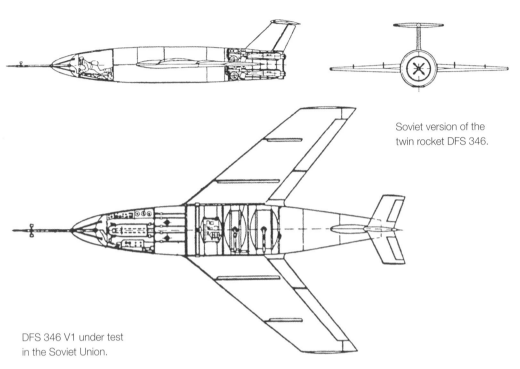

Soviet version of the
twin rocket DFS 346.

DFS 346 V1 under test
in the Soviet Union.

the Russians uprooted the entire 346 team and transferred them to a location 120km east of Moscow, where they set to work as if nothing untoward had happened other than a change of management. The Soviets then took things a step further, being obviously so generally impressed by what they saw at Halle that on 22 October 1946 they invited selected Siebel employees to come to the Soviet Union as guests for five years. Whether the response to the invitation was entirely voluntary is not known.

DFS test pilot Wolfgang Ziese, who was project pilot for the 346, had been captured at Halle and sent to Russia with the 346 team. There he was provided with two different gliders which Siebel had converted to prone position. Ziese was to keep in practice on these aircraft at Toplistan airfield, only 8km from the suburbs of Moscow. He was first called upon to make towed flights with the DFS 301 glider in the late summer of 1947 and these were completely successful.

Construction of the 346 was now confined to the twin rocket version and a 'detained' B-29 Superfortress was modified as its carrier. The first air-launched flight took place in early 1948 and reached 30,000ft before release from the mother aircraft. Ziese only lit one rocket but had to abort at a speed of some 1,100km/h because of fuselage vibration.

From 1949 the B-29 was replaced by a Russian Tu-4 and Ziese continued to make a series of test flights, during which it is almost certain the DFS 346 exceeded the speed of sound. But since it was neither a Russian aircraft nor pilot it received no public recognition in the Soviet Union.

The saga of the DFS 346 came to an end in the autumn of 1951 when Ziese was making a test flight at 60,000ft and a wing broke off. He kept his nerve in this dire situation and remained in his pressurised cockpit till the aircraft reached denser air at lower altitude, when he baled out and used his parachute to make a successful escape.

17 The eternal enigma

Dennis Bancroft, the
Chief Aerodynamicist
responsible for the M.52.

The core factor in the saga of the Miles M.52 is the enigma surrounding its cancellation. To this day no official definitive reason has been given, and to find out what the real reason might be is like preparing to enter a minefield of evasion. However, one man who probably had a more genuine desire to seek out the truth than anyone else is Dennis Bancroft, the Chief Aerodynamicist responsible for the M.52. He has devoted over fifty years of his life in determined pursuit of that objective. These are his findings.

It was well known that Frank Whittle had received many rebuffs from the Air Ministry since the late 1920s, and on many occasions had been very badly treated. It was only Whittle's tremendous determination and certainty that he alone was right which enabled him and Power Jets to achieve all that they did to give Britain the first reliable jet engine. No one could suggest that the Ministry had ever been very helpful in this matter. This lack of Ministry support meant that Whittle had, by necessity, been forced to fight through his personal ideas on the best way to achieve results ... and this approach is not the best way of making friends.

By 1943 the Government had at last realised that the jet engine was probably the engine of the future.

In April 1944 the Government nationalised Power Jets Ltd, Whittle being guaranteed that they would continue jet engine research, design and development. The main production would be taken over by the private engine-making firms.

By spring 1945 the main engine-production firms categori-
cally insisted that no design and development for complete
engines could be undertaken by Power Jets (R & D) Ltd, as that
would be unfair competition by a nationalised industry against
the private sector. Power Jets must only do detailed research and
development and not basic design. This had been the case with
RAE Farnborough, where the last aircraft designed by the then
Royal Aircraft Factory to go into production was during the
World War I (the BE-2). From then on – once the Royal Aircraft
Factory changed to the RAE – it gave the aircraft industry only
detailed research and development, and not overall designs.

By April 1945 the Ministry of Aircraft Production had agreed
this policy as being the only practical solution for Power Jets
and tried to put it into practice. However, this was completely
contrary to Whittle's approach – and also to the agreement made
at the formation of Power Jets (R & D) Ltd. Whittle was convinced that he and his team were the world leaders in the subject
and, indeed, 80% of the design of British jet engines in production at this time originated from the Whittle team.

During the rest of 1945 meetings and discussions were held,
but there was a complete impasse. Neither side would alter its
position which, of course, was completely opposed to the other's.

Whittle finally resigned from the Board of Power Jets (R & D)
Ltd with his letter of the 22 January 1946. But he continued his
campaign for what he thought was the best way to maintain
this country's lead in the development of the jet engine.

Air Marshal Sir Alec Coryton's (CRD) reply to Whittle on the
27 February 1946 put the Ministry's final, uncompromising
statement of their immovable resolve. During March the demise
of the original design team occurred and the sixteen key members of Whittle's original team resigned en bloc.

At this time the Ministry of Supply (on 7 August 1945 the
Ministry of Aircraft Production had merged with the Ministry of
Supply) was in a quandary. They had decided that there was no
alternative than to permit the powerful private sector aero-engine

manufacturers to have sole responsibility for the production and design and development of all jet engines. But they still had to deal with Whittle, a very well-known, active person, publicly esteemed as the inventor of the jet engine. For years Whittle had driven his ideas forward in spite of many Ministry rebuffs, but this Ministry decision was, in his opinion, the worst of all. He was prepared to do everything possible to reverse it.

Some people in the Ministry, therefore, were afraid of what would happen in the likely event of the M.52 flying supersonically in the latter part of 1946, powered by a unique Whittle engine. The enormous publicity which would undoubtedly occur on the occasion of the first manned flight through the sound barrier would seriously jeopardise the Ministry's decision to 'pension' Whittle off from all jet engine design work. In fact it would make it impossible to do so – and then where would they be?

The Ministry were in a difficult position. On one hand they had agreed with engine manufacturers that Whittle would not be permitted to design and develop any more jet engines at Power Jets (R & D) Ltd. On the other hand, a highly experienced influential man – whom the Ministry had agreed at the time of nationalising Power Jets could continue with engine design development – was to be stopped from doing so. He was prepared to raise Hell to try and reverse this injustice and the almost certain success of the Miles M.52 would dangerously fuel the flames.

The Ministry knew, from years of previous experience, that Whittle was a very determined man who would use any publicity to further his cause. At the moment the M.52 (E.24/43) project was classified as MOST SECRET, and nothing could be mentioned about it. However, as soon as the M.52 had broken the sound barrier, Britain would have to de-classify the project to get as much kudos as possible. The Ministry's and Whittle's flags would be flying high again, but what effect this would have on the Ministry's latest double-dealing with the private engine manufacturers can only be left to the imagination. A bright civil servant must have dreamt up the means of stopping Whittle from

Frank Whittle with
Sir Stafford Cripps,
Minister of Aircraft
Production, and
R. Dudley Williams.
On 24 October 1943
Whittle was told by
Sir Stafford that Power
Jets was to be taken
over by the State. On
28 April 1944 Power
Jets (Research and
Development) Ltd
was formed.

Whittle being invested
with the American
Legion of Honor by
General Ira C. Eaker
at the Pentagon on
15 November 1946.

recovering from the Ministry's latest devious dealings – by simply preventing Whittle's W.2/700 plus No. 4 Augmentor from being used to break the sound barrier.

It was only necessary for a sufficiently senior civil servant to cancel the project for some 'secret' reason for Whittle to be finally finished. Then the future jet engine manufacturing programme could run smoothly on with private engine firms designing, developing and producing engines. A new research and development group would be formed to work on jet engines, while Power Jets (R & D) Ltd would just employ one or two men to carry on the patent work. Whittle would thus be quietly removed to carry on his world-wide lecture tours.

The price to pay was to lose Britain the almost certain 'first' to fly through the sonic barrier and reach 1,000mph. But, of course, this was TOP SECRET – and who would know the truth for years to come or perhaps ever? It was essential that this – the real reason for the M.52 cancellation – did not become known, and the best way of keeping it secret was to circulate a number of different 'red herrings'. This may well be why the many different reasons for the cancellation have been given from time to time.

From the detailed evidence, which has taken over fifty years to accumulate, it will be seen conclusively that the Miles M.52 (E.24/43) was a completely sound concept and design – no one has produced any viable evidence to the contrary. Later information on supersonic flight has also consolidated this fact and no evidence for the M.52 not achieving at least 1,000mph has been found. This was the position at the time the contract was cancelled; any doubts would certainly have been used as the reason for cancellation in Sir Ben Lockspeiser's memo. Instead, the reasons given were feeble and very obviously false, and were known to be incorrect by Lockspeiser when he signed the cancellation memo of 20 February 1946 (see Appendix 7).

If Sir Ben actually thought that there was any technical reason why the M.52 would be unable to break the sound barrier, he was unaware of the true technological aspects of the contract.

Such ignorance on his part must be discounted as being impossible – he was the Ministry of Supply's Chief Scientist.

The main unknown factors at the time were the transonic dynamic problems of speed of centre of pressure movement versus aircraft inertia, and the optimum design for the engine air intake; only actual flight through the sound barrier could give the true answers. Much later transonic flight tests on other aircraft showed that the design choices made on the Miles M.52 would have proved completely satisfactory. Also, in October 1948, the one and only rocket drop-test of the model M.52 where the engine fired and did not blow up, demonstrated the model flying satisfactorily on autopilot and accelerating from 350 knots through the sound barrier to a speed of about 930mph (Mach 1.38) in level flight.

The decision made at the Supersonic Committee meeting of 12 February 1946 to change policy completely – from urgently wanting data on flying the M.52 transonically and supersonically to 1,000mph to suddenly having no interest in acquiring any such data – can only be for political expediency. No genuine technical reasons for the change of attitude exist. From their willingness to use the aircraft to test the engine it must be inferred that they considered the aircraft capable of obtaining supersonic speeds.

No written evidence of the real reason for the cancellation has been found, because no one would wish to put the real reason on paper and accept responsibility for the decision. The very strong – almost irresistible – circumstantial evidence for the reason for the cancellation was the urgent need to solve the major problem on jet engine design and development in which the Ministry was trapped – through their own mishandling of all parties – between the private sector engine manufacturers and Frank Whittle.

This cancellation of a project which had been handled with amazing speed and efficiency by both Miles Aircraft and Power Jets may have seemed a small price to pay, but it lost Britain the undoubted world lead in the supersonic field.

It is probable that the Supersonic Committee meeting of 12 February 1946 discussed the matter along these lines before unanimously agreeing the amazing statement that 'there was no case for continuing [the E.24/43 contract] on the grounds of obtaining information at transonic or supersonic speeds' (the reason for placing the contract). The members were all aware that the M.52 would almost certainly succeed in flying supersonically later that very year.

An alternative, and more honest, decision would have been to use the £400,000 or so wasted on the rocket-drop tests to offer a specific development contract to a new private firm to be set up by Whittle with private capital. This firm would develop and make jet engines – in a small way – which would not have upset the other private jet engine manufacturers and would, no doubt, have produced for this country some useful jet engine developments for the future. Then the Ministry would not have had to cancel the M.52 and give away our supersonic lead.

It took Britain almost another ten years from the cancellation of the contract before we produced the first experimental aircraft capable of 1,000mph. Surely the politicians could have found another way round the problem without sacrificing the world lead which Britain would almost certainly have held for years if only the Miles M.52 (E.24/43) contract had continued to fruition.

The Americans were amazed that Britain pulled out of supersonic flight by cancelling the M.52 at such a late stage. They appreciated that we were years ahead of them, both on airframe and engine design, and thought the M.52 was a winner. Earlier, to try and catch up, they were making the X-1, based more or less on the technical details of our know-how of the M.52 which had been passed on to them. But their lack of jet engine expertise was in the end such that they decided to go for a modified German rocket motor; it would take far too long to develop a suitable jet engine for the job. But then we just gave them the lead.

18 Guessing games

Dennis Bancroft's conspiracy theory is compelling in its logic, but it is his professional review of the potential of the M.52 which drives home the disastrous consequences of the loss by cancellation of that unique aircraft. Here is that review.

Hindsight is a great thing, and in the case of the M.52 the cancellation was a much more disastrous and expensive decision than even I or anyone else could have thought at the time. All our thoughts and efforts were directed to passing safely through the sonic barrier, which should have been achieved with the first M.52 in a shallow dive at the end of 1946, and flying level at 1,000mph, which should have been achieved with the second M.52, fitted with No. 4 Augmentor and afterburning, by the summer of 1947.

Normally, the drag of an aircraft increases more rapidly with speed than the thrust, whether propeller or jet-driven. But the Miles M.52 engine/airframe combination had the unique feature that, while at about Mach 1.2 the engine thrust equalled the aircraft drag, as the speed increased the thrust increased faster than the drag. This, in fact, gives an unstable forward speed characteristic and if the engine throttle is left set, the aircraft just increases speed at an ever-faster rate until the engine overheats, or, if an efficient jet restricter was designed, then the speed would increase until the aircraft itself overheated.[1] This longitudinal speed instability is unique, and although a simple control between A.S.I. and throttle could have been fitted, it was considered that warning any experienced test pilot of this unique

1. Aluminium aircraft are limited to about Mach 2.2 because of temperature rise generated by the compression of the air.

feature would be adequate. He could control the maximum speed he wished to achieve, as mere temperature was the ultimate speed limitation of this aircraft and not the drag. The maximum speed to which we considered it safe to go would be ascertained from flight tests, the jet nozzle size, engine temperature and duct strength determining the first limiting speed of 1,000mph.

This longitudinal excess of thrust over drag at 1,000mph is quite large and was estimated to give about $\frac{1}{3}$g acceleration. This means that if the engine is not throttled back at – say – 1,000mph the aircraft speed would be increasing at about 400mph per minute and the aircraft would soon self-destruct.

This feature of the aircraft/engine combination is entirely due to the ram-jet effect of the engine. At the time we never even considered the full significance of this unique feature. Now, it is obvious that once having achieved 1,000mph our sights would be set on greater and greater speeds, and the only limitation was the stress/temperature characteristics of materials. For example, between the time the M.52 was started and the time it was can-celled, a new turbine blade material, Nimonic 90, had been developed and the basic W.2/700 static thrust had been increased by 25% from 2,000 to 2,500lb. The use of normal aircraft light alloys to construct the airframe, and perspex for the canopy, would have limited the first aircraft to a Mach of about 2 – i.e. 1,325mph, the same as the Concorde. But as the specification was only for 1,000mph, in the interests of saving weight, there was an engine duct pressure restriction corresponding to Mach 1.5 at 36,000ft – i.e. 1,000mph. With a small weight increase, this pressure restriction could have been raised virtually to whatever was required. Replacing the perspex canopy with glass would permit a speed increase to some 2,000mph – Mach 3.

But one has to face the increased strength needed to be built into the airframe to counteract the increasing weakness of alu-minium as a result of the heat rising as the speed goes up. A variable restrictor would have to be fitted to keep the engine temperatures down, but the use of stainless steel leading edges

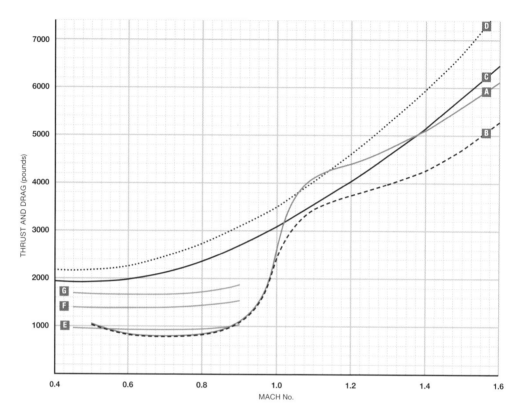

Total drag and thrusts of the M.52 at 36,000ft with the W.2/700 engine and No. 4 Augmentor with Nimonic 90 blades; bypass exhaust nozzle area 3.6sq ft.

A graph based on a paper written by Dennis Bancroft in 1997. The original source of some of the curves is the last Miles M.52 report written by Bancroft in March 1945 (PE.52/1) in which he estimates the performance of the aircraft. Some of the material has been omitted, and there are additions. Curve B is an interpretation of the lower drag figures from the RAE report on the flight of the Vickers rocket-propelled model. Curves E, F and G are the thrust figures for other contemporary jet engines.

A Total drag estimate / 1945.

B Total drag estimate calculated from rocket model drop test data, obtained 9 October 1948.

C Thrust produced by W.2/700 + No. 4 Augmentor at 17,600rpm, using Nimonic 90 blades; estimated by Power Jets in 1945.

D Thrust produced by W.2/700 + No. 4 Augmentor at 10° below ICAN conditions.

E Thrust produced by Rolls-Royce Derwent (1945).

F Thrust produced by Rolls-Royce Nene (1945).

G Thrust produced by Rolls-Royce Avon (1945).

and nose cone would enable the throttle to be left fully open for a little longer to achieve the next highest safe speed.

This continuing development of the same basic design, which always allowed it to experiment at speeds greater than any other aircraft of its day at a relatively low cost, would have been invaluable for years – and perhaps even to the present day. Any new material, etc., developed could be tested relatively cheaply with this machine. The unique feature of always having more thrust than drag at higher speeds produces an immensely valuable experimental tool.

Could not the basic engine/fuselage combination have been used for years to test, speedily and economically, the supersonic performance of new wing sections, plan forms and controls, etc.? Miles Aircraft had for years made and tested the full-scale low-speed characteristics of wing sections and flaps, etc., by fitting special wings and components to an existing Miles aircraft to carry out the early full-scale tests. The unique engine, giving ever-increasing thrust with speed and weighing only about 1,200lb, with a variable exit nozzle and the availability of titanium from 1948 onwards, would be capable of giving a supersonic thrust well over ten times its weight. It is understood that, to this day, no other jet engine can come near to matching this.

Apart from the suitable engine characteristics for faster and faster supersonic testing, the design of the fuselage of the M.52 would have been admirably suited to further flight testing of other wings and components.

The fuselage basically consisted of a very large-diameter tube from nose to tail, to take the pilot's pressurised cabin at the front and to house, without any internal struts, etc., the standard engine and a very large duct for the No. 4 Augmentor and large exhaust nozzle. This free, tubular area was surrounded by special – very large and strong – machined rings to take all the wing bending moments and controls, etc., and to leave uncluttered the enormous clear tubular area from end to end in the fuselage. This means that almost any external wing or control shape could be used in place of the existing units by simply joining up to the existing stress-carrying unions.

The fuselage was substantially 'self-contained', including fuel tanks and undercarriage. Really, an ideal basis for change of components for test purposes, although this aspect had not been considered in the original M.52 design specification.

It must be emphasised that all this refers to experimental test flying for development purposes – as the M.52 had always been – and not production military or civil aircraft, where requirements are different and fuel economy is of much greater importance.

Using a 50-year-old design for experimental work is by no means novel. For instance, it is understood that all new basic development work on ejector seats in this country is carried out on a Meteor, an aircraft designed at that same period. But it might be considered amazing that the potentially fastest aircraft in the world could still basically have been a 50-year-old design, and with a pilot-ejection system most probably safer for very high-speed escape than those fitted to present-day aircraft. What have we thrown away?

As a literary team we do not all share the same conspiracy view-point, and the Miles Aircraft Collection representatives believe the reason for the E.24/43 cancellation was a relatively simple one – post-war Britain was bankrupt and the M.52 was a spi-ralling cost luxury we simply could not afford. The question of the cancellation was not discussed in Parliament as there is no record of it in Hansard, nor was it discussed in Cabinet meet-ings; there is no mention of it in the Cabinet Secretary's hand-written notebooks for the period covering October 1945 to April 1946.

Peter Amos and Josh Spoor are therefore forced to the in-escapable conclusion that the M.52 was cancelled simply on mis-guided grounds of economy. Although Sir Ben Lockspeiser was seen to have finally been responsible for announcing the cancel-lation, he could not have taken the decision himself. He was responsible to the Minister of Supply and Aircraft Production, John Wilmot, and it is with the latter that the buck must rest.

Personally I have a quite different slant on the likely cause of the cancellation. Based as I was at the RAE in Farnborough, I was heavily involved in the preparations to enter Germany on the fall of the Third Reich and was a member of the Farren Mission set up to evaluate the advanced aviation technology we anticipated finding in that country. What we actually found exceeded our wildest expectations and rocked the aviation world back on its heels.

When this treasure trove of wind tunnels, new aerodynamic shapes, axial flow jet engines, rocketry, weaponry, ejection seats and much more was analysed, and the engineers, designers and test pilots who created and tested them were interrogated, the aviation world was forced to pause and absorb it all. There was a distinct feeling of entering a new era in aviation history which would affect the whole course, not only of military aviation. There would be a new impetus to civil aviation now that hostilities had ceased and peace once more reigned.

Dr G.P. Douglas, the head of the Aerodynamics Department at RAE Farnborough.

The RAE was drenched with this new atmosphere, for a large number of its scientists and pilots had been to Germany to experience for themselves first hand what was on offer. On returning, a plethora of meetings was held to analyse what had been found of aeronautical value and how this might affect both present and future experiments. Inevitably in the Aerodynamics Department the M.52 came under scrutiny in this respect, and although no support for it was withdrawn at that stage, it was clear that some ambivalence about certain aspects of the project was felt by Dr G.P. Douglas, the head of department. He was an ex-RFC pilot who had lost a leg in World War I, and was now a member of the Supersonic Committee. He had obviously been very impressed by what he had seen in post-war Germany.

At such meetings that I attended at RAE, Morien Morgan, the head of the Aero Flight Section, always gave a clear picture of the progress being made at Woodley and his support for the M.52 never appeared to waver. However, in mid-December 1945 he and I drove to Woodley for a Miles meeting. On the way back to Farnborough he expressed some of his concerns about the state of progress of the W.2/700, especially in the light of the unrest at Power Jets. He was really quite worried about the risk of not having a fully developed and reliable engine for the high-speed tests, since he felt an engine failure could be catastrophic for the pilot. I listened of course, but countered that it was the nature of our profession to accept such risks and we left it at that, but I could see he was disturbed on this issue.

As the year 1945 slipped away I had an instinctive feeling that the wind of change was blowing through British, and indeed world, aviation as designers began to turn to German technology and new aircraft shapes appeared on drawing boards. Was the 1943 shape of the M.52 now regarded as outdated? Perhaps so in the minds of the Supersonic Committee, but we shall never know.

But if they hadn't cancelled the M.52 and spent the money on the rocket-model contract, which itself was cancelled immediately after the only successful flight, with little additional information obtained, the Ministry would have achieved piloted, supersonic flight for far less money than the cost of the rocket-model contract alone, and I might have been the first pilot to break the sound barrier.

Postscript

Some little time after writing this chapter I was reflecting on what was said, when something stirred in my memory box and took me back to April 1945. As the Third Reich was in its death throes, the Americans, like us, were preparing to pour their experts into Germany to probe its aviation technological secrets. No one was more keen to exploit this potential treasure trove than General H.H. 'Hap' Arnold, the supremo of the USAAF, who had long recognised its technological shortcomings.

Arnold had already been made alive to this when in March 1941 he learned that the Gloster E.28/39, Britain's first jet aircraft, was about to fly. He was given access to Whittle's work, and quickly had the Whittle W.1X engine shipped to the USA to be built under licence by General Electric, thus pushing America into the Jet Age. Arnold indeed was no slouch and he reacted with similar rapidity to the situation pending with the defeat of Germany in 1945, by forming in late 1944 the AAF Scientific Advisory Group, headed by Dr Theodore von Karman.

Dr von Karman was a world renowned aerodynamicist of Hungarian nationality, who had studied in Germany before emigrating to the USA. In the 1930s he had been director of the Guggenheim Aeronautical Laboratory at California Institute of Technology. He arrived in Britain on his latest mission in April 1945 and made contact with the British Farren Mission,[1] which

1. In early 1945 the Ministry of Aircraft Production set up the Farren Mission, named after W.S. Farren, Director of the RAE Farnborough, to seek out the aviation advanced technology secrets in post-war Germany. The Mission was comprised of RAE scientists and test pilots.

OPPOSITE:
General 'Hap' Arnold, head of the US Army Air Corps, with Air Chief Marshal Wilfrid Freeman, the RAF Vice-Chief of Air Staff. Arnold was well aware of the US technological short-comings and was determined to exploit the aviation secrets which became available with the defeat of Germany.

Dr Theodore von Karman, the world renowned Hungarian aerodynamicist, was impressed by Eric Brown's confidence that the M.52 would break the sound barrier. He no doubt warned Arnold that Britain was likely to achieve this before the USAAF.

was tasked with a similar quest to his own, and of which I was a member. We met on an informal basis at the Royal Aeronautical Society in London, and at one stage he took me aside and asked about the flying of captured enemy piston-engine aircraft at RAE Farnborough, but then moved over to the subject of the M.52. This surprised me somewhat, and his emphasis was on a possible projected date to attempt the breaking of the sound barrier, and whether I was confident of success. My positive enthusiasm for the M.52 seemed to take him aback somewhat, and was doubtless conveyed to General Arnold.

Many years later I learned that one of General Arnold's life ambitions was to form a United States Air Force (USAF) independent from the United States Army Air Force (USAAF). He wanted the changeover date to coincide with a world attention-getting aviation event, and he had set as his goal the breaking of the sound barrier. Therefore in 1945/46 the M.52 loomed as a threat to his plans. So here we have the elements to form a conspiracy theory. At the end of World War II Britain was financially bankrupt, so why not use the United States' formidable finances to buy out the M.52 and prevent it raining on General Arnold's parade. Far fetched and a slur on our gallant allies – perhaps not, as I was to experience. Before the end of World War II the Allies had decided that after the capitulation Germany would be divided into four Occupation Zones. In the British Zone was the Hermann Goering Aeronautical Research Centre at Völkenrode which was overrun by American troops on 13 April 1945. It was located near Brunswick, had a 3,000ft grass runway attached to it, and consisted of six institutes carrying out advanced aeronautical experiments with the aid of seven wind tunnels of varying sizes and speeds.

Whittle's W.IX engine which Arnold shipped to the USA, to be built under licence by General Electric, thus hoisting the USA into the Jet Age.

The Americans, realising this would be a jewel in the crown of the Farren Mission, hurriedly installed a US Exploitation Division team, led by Colonel Donald Putt, which systematically plundered the facilities, removing loads of data and equipment both by road and by air before the British arrived in June. Removal of the major items by air was done clandestinely at night by a B-17 Flying Fortress and a B-24 Liberator put at Colonel Putt's disposal.

At the Potsdam Conference (17 July to 2 August) the British uttered a strong complaint about the Völkenrode incidents, but they fell on the deaf ears of General Arnold. Whatever the real facts are underlying the cancellation of the M.52, one thing is certain and that is that the formation of the new USAF and the Bell X-1's breaking of the sound barrier both took place, as planned, on 14 October 1947. Also, let it be noted, Donald Putt did not receive his reward in heaven, but in a grateful USAF where he rose to Lieutenant General.

As if to underscore the possibility of a financial deal having been done over the M.52 between Britain and the USAF, there no longer exists any records attributable to John Wilmot, the Government Minister of Supply and Aircraft Production at the relevant time. How could there be absolutely no traceable evidence of Mr Wilmot's term of office?

There can be no smoke without fire!

Appendices

APPENDIX 1

Preliminary note on Miles-Power Jets very high-speed aircraft by Group Captain Frank Whittle
23 October 1943

INTRODUCTION

This is an experimental aircraft, the purpose of which is to explore the possibilities of flight at speeds in the range 600–1,000mph.

POWER PLANT

The power plant is to be a W.2/700 type JP engine and No. 4 design ducted fan, with provision for further heating of the output of the ducted fan. A final decision has not yet been made as between:

(1) The ducted fan and its driving turbine exhausting into a common duct.

(2) The exhaust from the fan turbine and the fan being separated up to the propelling nozzle.

Both schemes have advantages and disadvantages which have not yet been fully examined.

It is expected that the power plant will provide sufficient power to propel the aircraft up to speeds between 500 and 600mph without the use of the supplementary combustion chambers (in the duct behind the fan) but that this additional heating will be required for take-off and the higher speeds.

A preliminary examination indicates that though a much greater rate of climb can be obtained by the use of supplementary heating there is little difference in the amount of fuel used in reaching 40,000ft.

FUEL LOAD

The amount of fuel to be carried is to be sufficient to reach a height of 40,000ft and to permit half-an-hour's flight at 700mph at that height.

It is not possible to estimate the amount of fuel required for this but it is assessed at approximately 2,000lb, i.e. about 40 cu ft.

USEFUL LOAD

The aircraft has to carry a pilot and all the special instruments required for obtaining the information desired, including an automatic observer. It is assumed that this part of the weight should be represented by about 500lb.

ALL-UP WEIGHT

This is estimated to be 6,000–6,500lb. The lower figure should be attainable if (say) 500lb of the fuel is looked upon as overload, and if the maximum ASI is restricted to (say) 400mph.

UNDERCARRIAGE

The take-off thrust should be of the order of two-thirds or more of the all-up weight. It may therefore be possible to dispense with wheels and use skids. If this course is considered undesirable then a tricycle undercarriage will have to be used in order to keep the jet blast off the runway during take-off. This should be made as short as possible in order to keep down the weight and reduce the problem of stowage. If sufficiently short it might be more desirable to use a fixed undercarriage with retractable fairing, i.e. streamline covers are retracted for landing and take-off.

THE DUCT

The fuselage layout is dominated by the requirements for the power plant ducts. If a single intake at the nose is to be used then in order to get high ram efficiency at speeds of the order of 500mph it will require to be 3ft in diameter. The duct velocity would then be about 200ft/sec. The overall diameter of the W.2/700 is about 42in so that in order to provide an annular space sufficiently large to permit the fan air to pass without appreciable loss the diameter of the portion of the duct which contains the engine would have to be about 4ft 6in.

The diameter of the ducted fan is likely to be of the order of 42in. After the fan the duct should be as large as possible so as to keep the average air velocity low in the portion of the duct occupied by the supplementary combustion chambers in order to keep the combustion chamber pressure loss as low as possible.

The final nozzle will have to be variable in size, and if circular its diameter would need to be about 21in without supplementary heating and about 29in with it.

The duct therefore will consist of a front portion of about 3ft diameter diverging to about 4½ft in the region of the engine then converging to 3½ft at the fan, with possibly a divergence (such as the layout will permit) in the region of the supplementary combustion chambers, with eventual convergence to about 2¾ft immediately forward of the final nozzle.

FUSELAGE LAYOUT

This is a very thorny problem. The duct is so bulky that the maximum diameter of the fuselage cannot be much less than 5ft.

The most difficult problem is the disposition of the power plant, pilot, instruments, etc., and fuel, to obtain a reasonable position of the c.g. In general the most satisfactory arrangement seems to be to have the pilot and instruments right at the front, with the main engine a little forward of mid-fuselage, and to split the fuel tank into two portions, one forward and the other aft of the main engine compartment. With this arrangement it will be necessary to ensure that the fuel is drawn from both tanks simultaneously so that the c.g. of the fuel does not move as fuel is consumed. The fuel tanks in this arrangement would most conveniently be in the form of annular containers round the duct.

If the forward portion of the duct is a single 3ft diameter tube then it is very difficult to stow the pilot, nose wheel, etc., without very large protuberances. This might be avoided by using four 18in diameter ducts with the pilot sitting between them.

If the circular section is departed from in the duct substantial structure weight would have to be added in order to stiffen the non-circular walls against the duct pressures.

If excessive structure weight in the fuselage is to be avoided it seems essential to make the duct the foundation of the fuselage structure, except at the after part where the wall of the duct would be subject to high temperatures. Thus it is proposed that the main structure of the fuselage would consist of the duct wall and the outer skin plus supporting hoops and stringers. The portions of the duct where changes of cross section take place will have to be designed with the duct pressure as the main consideration.

LAYOUT – GENERAL

Whatever arrangement is used it seems inevitable that the c.g. will be somewhere about mid fuselage. It seems therefore likely that the conventional arrangement of main-plane and tailplane will have to be abandoned in favour of a tandem arrangement in which the two sets of lifting surfaces approximately share the load.

With the tandem arrangement it is not possible to stow the undercarriage in the wing. If a retractable undercarriage is used it will therefore have to be retracted into the fuselage. The only feasible place seems to be the portion of the fuselage where the duct converges from 4½ft to 3½ft diameter.

For the high speeds contemplated very thin wings are desirable. A tandem arrangement should help in this direction but even so there seems to be a strong case for some multi-plane arrangement.

THE TANDEM TRIPLANE

If one imagines a biplane with a very big taper then it is possible to converge the wings while keeping a reasonable gap:chord ratio. In the limit, if the wings are triangular in plan form, they can meet at the tip and be mutually supporting structurally. If one goes a step further and imagines a triplane in which the third plane is midway between the other two planes in height but staggered back longitudinally then we have a pyramid arrangement if all three planes join at their tips, which should be extremely strong structurally.

The tandem triplane proposed consists of six pairs of planes. The mid-planes of the rear group may conveniently fulfil the function of elevators and the mid-planes of the forward group that of ailerons. We thus have control surfaces without fixed surfaces immediately in front of them.

The arrangement described should make it possible to use wings of the order of 5% thick and of very low structure weight. It is estimated that the structure weight of the wings would be of the order of 5% of all-up weight as compared with the more usual figure of about 14%. This should more than compensate for the fact that the total lifting surface would require to be of the order of 10% more than that of the equivalent orthodox aeroplane.

For the aircraft under consideration it is estimated that the root:chord of the wings in this arrangement would be about 3ft and that the span would be 23ft, giving a net wing loading of the order of 40lb/sq.ft.

DRAG

The bulk of the fuselage is such that the wetted surface is of the order of twice that of the wings. It seems unlikely therefore that the value of CDo will be less than 0.025.

It is estimated that a fixed undercarriage with fairing retractable for take-off and landing would add about 8% to the total wetted surface which might be compensated by the general weight reduction associated with it.

APPENDIX 2

Memorandum from Norbert Rowe, Director of Technical Development, to Air Marshal Ralph Sorley, Controller of Research and Development at the Ministry of Aircraft Production. 11 November 1943

I gave you a brief verbal account of my meeting with Miles at Reading on 6/11/43, when we discussed his designs for the high-speed aircraft with his staff, DSP, DDSR1, DD/RDA and representatives of Power Jets.

The firm have evolved a very attractive layout shown in the folder immediately behind this file. You will note the very large body and the small wing. This is necessary to induct all the air required for the W.2/700 engine with afterburning behind a ducted fan. DDSR1 has asked that the question of the optimum power plant be critically examined from the standpoint of thrust, less drag, and the RAE will do this as quickly as possible. It may turn out that there is a better balance of thrust over drag with a smaller diameter engine without afterburning, and hence, with a much smaller diameter body.

You will note the implications of the high priority Miles expects when applied to a project of this sort. It affects not only materials and labour but runs over to other firms already deeply committed and to extensive wind tunnel tests at NPL and RAE, as set out in the separate sheet within the attached folder. I think the project merits very high priority, but we shall have to watch the situation very carefully to ensure that other urgent things more directly related to war activities are not prejudiced.

I think the firm has shown, by the way they have tackled the initial stages, that we could safely entrust this project to them, and I would like your agreement to the placing of the contract for two prototypes and parts for a third, and also your concurrence in the high priority Miles asks for.

APPENDIX 3

Memorandum from Dr H.M. Garner, Deputy Director, SR1, Ministry of Aircraft Production to Norbert Rowe, Director of Technical Development. 3 January 1944

As a result of discussions at DSR's Supersonic Committee on 14 December and with Miles Aircraft on 20 December (enc. 16A), there is some change in the proposals laid down in my letter of 1 December (enc. 11B). The committee decided that as for wings of 7½% thick or less the behaviour at low speeds was, according to wind tunnel tests, hardly affected by the shape of the section and in view of the advantage of a sharp leading edge at high speeds a wing with this feature was desirable.

This brings back the importance of tests of wings on the Falcon and these are being arranged (16A). Tests on all-moving power-operated tailplane on the Spitfire are also being arranged (enc. 16A).

APPENDIX 4

Memorandum from J.E. Serby, Deputy Director, Research and Development Administration to Dr H.M. Garner, Deputy Director, SR1, Ministry of Aircraft Production. 2 August 1944

If Tech Note Aero 1470 is correct then more importance attaches, than before, to the conventional wings. We were previously thinking of making these by building fairings on to the biconvex wings, but they should now be built as proper wings to the conventional profile as it may be that we shall do most of our work with them.

You may have plans in hand for this.

APPENDIX 5

Memorandum from Dr H.M. Garner, Deputy Director, SR1, Ministry of Aircraft Production to J.E. Serby, Deputy Director, Research and Development Administration. 4 August 1944

We had a long discussion on this at our meeting on 28 July and decided to go ahead with the supersonic wings but to have wings with rounded leading edges as a second string. Miles and RAE are to discuss the latter and I am not sure whether they will be modified supersonic wings or conventional. I am not sure what weight should be attached to Aero 1470 in view of the low Reynolds number.

APPENDIX 6

The Churchill Directive
Priorities for Research and Development
Note by the Prime Minister, 15 January 1945

At the present stage of the war research and development projects likely to be effectively used in operations before the end of 1946 must have the highest priority.

Research workers and draughtsmen are scanty and are needed also by industry in preparation for the change-over to peace-time production and for the development of civil air transport.

All Service research and development projects now in hand must, therefore, be reviewed forthwith in the light of current hypotheses about the end of the German War and the duration of the Japanese War. Those which are not likely to be used in operations on a considerable scale in the second half of 1946 should be slowed down or temporarily abandoned so as to permit the maximum concentration upon the remainder and some release of man-power to civilian production.

Departments must also review their present practice in making modifications, particularly to obsolescent weapons and equipment (including aircraft), so as to cut out all but those which are essential for operational purposes or to save life. This replaces my directive of the 16 February 1943. W.P. (43)54.

W.S.C.

10 Downing Street, S.W.1.

APPENDIX 7

Memorandum from Sir Ben Lockspeiser, Chairman of the Supersonics Committee to Air Commodore G. Silyn Roberts, Director of the Armaments Research Department. 20 February 1946

We must cut our losses and cancel the contract on this aircraft. The matter was fully discussed at the last meeting of the Supersonic Cte and I have subsequently discussed the matter with the firm. There will be no tears anywhere except perhaps at PJs – but we are not paying £250,000 to test an engine.

I believe the conception behind the decision to build this aircraft was to get supersonic information. We now know that was putting the cart before the horse. No more supersonic aircraft till our rocket-propelled models & wind tunnels have given us enough information to proceed on a reliable basis.

Copy to Air Marshal Ralph Sorley, Controller of Research and Development at the Ministry of Aircraft Production

APPENDIX 8
Miles E.24/43: Latest known aerodynamics data
Spring 1946

The following information is the best available at the time of the cancellation of the E.24/43 contract in the spring of 1946. After that the Vickers contract for the one-third scale M.52 rocket models continued until the only successful telemetered flight was made on the 9 October 1948. This one and only successful flight before the contract was cancelled was described in the RAE's 1950 report on these tests, R & M 2835 'Flight Trials of a Rocket-Propelled Transonic Research Model'. This single 55-second, rocket-firing flight gave a considerable amount of information during its satisfactory 90 or so mile flight, including a once and for all contradiction of Mr Smelt's insistence that the increase of drag in the transonic range was some 10 or 20 times, based on his extrapolation of his *sub*-sonic windtunnel tests. The RAE report on the successful model's flight clearly confirms Dr Maccoll's results that the increase in supersonic drag of the M.52 would only have been two to four times, and these were the figures we believed and always used in our drag calculations. In fact, using the data given in RAE report R & M 2835 shows that our overall drag estimate was some 10% *pessimistic*. Reducing our overall drag estimate by some 10% would almost certainly make the need for any small, shallow dive unnecessary. At 36,000ft the M.52 would be able to fly level at any speed between subsonic climbing speed and supersonic 1,000mph.

A.U.W. First aircraft: W.2/700 only, having 18-inch diameter exhaust nozzle and 200 gals. fuel: 6,763lb

Second aircraft: W.2/700 + No. 4 Augmentor, etc. Exhaust nozzle 3.6sq ft area (26-inch diameter); normal maximum loading with 200 gals: 7,861lb Overload 250 gals: 8,211lb

Gross wing area: 142sq ft
Net wing area: 108.7sq ft

Span: 26.875ft

Mean chord: 5.28ft

Aspect ratio: 5.09

Root section: constant radius, 7½% biconvex

Tip section: constant radius, 4.02% biconvex

Wing loading: Second aircraft, normal loading (200 gals) 55.4 lb/sq ft

First aircraft with 100 gals 42.7 lb/sq ft

Plain flaps

Dive recovery flaps (mounted on fuselage below the wing, hinging out spanwise about the 50% chord position): 3 in. deep × 12 in. long.

Tailplane
  gross area: 53.5 sq ft
  net area: 35.9 sq ft
  C.P. position at low speed: 18% – 23% S.M.C.
  span (tip to tip): 15.98 ft
  mean chord: 3.3 ft
  root section: constant radius, 6% biconvex
  tip section: constant radius, 3.9% biconvex

Fin and rudder
  area: 18.5 sq ft
  height (mid-chord line): 4.58 ft
  mean chord: 4.04 ft
  root section: constant radius, 7.5% biconvex
  tip section: constant radius, 4.48% biconvex

Flying controls
  rudder: ± 15°

  all-moving tailplane – angular movement (though this is expected to be reduced after flight test experience): 8° up and down

  aileron (with provision for modification as dictated by flight tests): 9° up and 6° down

Fuselage
  overall length: 35ft 7.22in
  maximum diameter: 5ft
  thickness ratio: .140
  wetted area: 443sq ft

Pressure cabin: volume of cabin: 36 cu ft

Fuel system: C.G. of fuel system = 26% S.M.C. maintained in *all conditions of flight*, using metering device to withdraw ▬▬)ortionate amounts from each of five tanks.

Tank capacities
  First three annular tanks:
  Tank 1   50 gals
  Tank 2   39 gals
  Tank 3   52 gals

  Annular, round jet pipe:
  Tank 4   30 gals

  Saddle type:
  Tank 5   79 gals
                          ─────────────
                                250 gals

Normal maximum capacity to meet specification = 200 gals
Overload to 250 gals if required for special tests.

Power plant: thrusts as estimated by Power Jets and confirmed to Miles, spring 1946.

  First aircraft with W.2/700 only (18in exhaust nozzle), static thrust: 2,500lb

  Second aircraft with W.2/700 + No. 4 Augmentor, etc., exhaust nozzle area: 3.6sq ft (26-in. diameter), thrust at 36,000ft: 6,950lb

  With Nimonic 90 (high-nickel alloy) blades at air temperature 10° below normal ICAN, which, at 1,000mph is equivalent to ..... Developed h.p. of 18,500

Performance:

First aircraft with W.2/700 only (18in exhaust nozzle), maximum speed at 30,000ft: 585mph

Second aircraft with W.2/700 + No. 4 Augmentor, etc. (3.6sq ft, 26in diameter, exhaust nozzle), maximum speed at sea level (limited by power plant limit at sea level due to maximum pressure permitted in engine duct: 700mph. Maximum speed at 36,000ft: 1,000mph (see Note 1) Best climbing speed: 600mph Take-off distance to 50ft: 4,560ft

Note 1. This maximum speed is limited by power plant temperature limitation and *not* by thrust available at 1,000mph, which would, in fact, be greater than the drag. By reducing the exhaust nozzle area a little the maximum speed of the aircraft could be increased considerably before the engine reached its temperature limit, but at the expense of a small reduction of available thrust at all speeds. Early flight tests would show the best exhaust nozzle area for specific test flights. The initial area chosen was to give the specification 1,000mph, and may have required a small, shallow dive between approximately 700 and 750mph to reach the higher range of flying continuously in the speed range of 750 to 1,000mph. But early flight tests and nozzle design adjustment was the only way of finding the best compromise.

APPENDIX 9

Extract from White Paper 'The Supply of Military Aircraft' presented to Parliament in February 1955

RESEARCH

6. The decision was also taken in 1946 that, in the light of the limited knowledge then available, the risks of attempting supersonic flight in manned aircraft were unacceptably great and that our research into the problems involved should be conducted in the first place by means of air-launched models. It is easy to be wise after the event, but it is clear now that this decision seriously delayed the progress of aeronautical research in the UK.

APPENDIX 10
Definitive list of M.52 models to various scales, by D.S. Bancroft, March 2000

Taylor's Report R & M 1467, of April 1932, gave Ackeret's mathematical analysis of the drag of supersonic wings, and the fact that double wedge and bi-convex wings gave significantly lower supersonic drags. For the M.52 project to be successful, the minimum supersonic drag of all the components was necessary. However, although it was thought that the supersonic information given in this Report was substantially correct, there was absolutely no information on how such wing sections would behave at normal, subsonic speeds. Therefore, at the end of 1943, one of the first urgent jobs on the M.52 project was to make a parallel section of a 7½% thick bi-convex wing (Model No. 1) and test it in the Miles windtunnel to see if such a wing section could be made to fly at subsonic speeds and take off and land satisfactorily. The bi-convex wing was chosen because, although the double wedge section at the same thickness/chord ratio gave a slightly smaller drag, the very important wing stiffness requirement permitted a smaller thickness/chord wing of bi-convex section, as the stiffness was proportional to the greater enclosed cross-sectional area of the section, thus giving lower wing drag.

Model No. 1: Parallel section 7½% thick bi-convex, approx. 4ft span and 12in. chord, made of Jabroc. Tests were made at speeds of 100–150mph and showed that a reasonable flow over the surface was obtained and the maximum C_L of 0.78 was achieved, showing that the wing was satisfactory for subsonic operation.

Model No. 2: From the results of the above it was decided that a flying aeroplane would be needed to test the full-scale bi-convex wing in order to check the subsonic flying characteristics and to measure the full-scale wing drag, and thus the GILLETTE FALCON was inaugurated. It was proposed that the Falcon, initially, should only have a full-scale bi-convex wing, with its own orthodox tailplane and elevator. In fact, the Falcon was fitted with split flaps as standard, not plain flaps as finally chosen for the M.52. Flights proved satisfactory.

Model No. 3: As the next stage was to fit the bi-convex tail-plane and elevator to the Falcon, this had first to be tested in the windtunnel. A windtunnel model was therefore made and tested, being a parallel bi-convex tailplane and elevator, span 49in., chord 11.5in., area 3.9ft^2, 7½% T/C. This was made of Jabroc. Windtunnel results were satisfactory, and the full-scale version was therefore fitted to the Falcon. After several flight tests, the Falcon was then fitted with an all-moving tailplane.

Model No. 4: Parallel wing section with 25% chord plain flap. Span 55.8in., chord 12.45in. area 4.85ft^2, 7.25% T/C. Made of mahogany. Although the full-scale Falcon wing was provided with the standard split flap, for both structural and drag reasons a plain flap was considered desirable for the M.52 itself, and therefore this model was made and tested. However, for a comparison to the full-scale/model results, this model was also provided with an optional, additional split flap, which could be fitted to the model when the plain flaps were in neutral. This enabled a correlation between the model and the full-scale flaps on the Falcon to be obtained.

Model No. 5: A range of full-scale models or 'mock-ups' was made, initially in a small hut on the aerodrome close to the Experimental Department, where work was concentrated initially on the cockpit, as the space for the pilot was so limited and a large air-intake for the engine had to be provided. Initially, the air-intake consisted of the more normal, elliptical side entries, somewhat similar in appearance to the

Harrier. The first two cockpits covered variants of this entry. However, it was agreed with Power Jets that, due to the unknown problems associated with an efficient supersonic air-intake for an engine with a completely circular cockpit, a complete annular air-intake with internal control flaps was likely to provide a better and more controllable solution. The third 'mock-up' cockpit was along these lines, and then a 'mock-up' of the remainder of the fuselage and tail-unit was required, but became too big to be produced in the small hut and was therefore transferred to a partitioned-off section of the Experimental Department. It is interesting to note that whereas 'mock-ups' are normally used to give a general guidance to shape, etc., it was found that, owing to the amount of structure, equipment and controls, etc., which had to be fitted into the annular ring of the fuselage between the enormous jet-pipe and the small external diameter of the fuselage, all the small members of the 'mock-up' were made from rectangular pieces of wood to precisely the overall maximum dimensions of the bent-metal stringers, etc., from which the final aircraft would be constructed. The full development of the final 'mock-up' model continued over the whole period of development of the aircraft.

Model No. 6: By the spring of 1944, the final general design of the aircraft had been completed, and a windtunnel model was required for the Miles windtunnel for comprehensive tests of airflow, drag, stability, etc. A 1:6.154 scale model was therefore constructed with a span of 4.4ft. The Experimental Department made this model with an aluminium alloy fuselage and Jabroc wing and tail sections, as this material would be strong enough for the 100–150mph wind speed normally used in our tunnel.

Model No. 7: Clothed parallel wing for fuel tank. Span 4.65ft, wing area 6.2ft^2, wing chord 1.33ft. This model was made so that windtunnel tests could be done to check the feasibility of using an additional fuel tank during take-off and climb, as well as improving the L/D ratio of the wing by giving it a more orthodox shape for take-off and climb.

Model No. 8: Supersonic model. The fuselage was turned from brass, with all-steel wing and tail units, approx. 1:36 scale, span approx, 9in. This was made specially to fit into the largest NPL supersonic windtunnel after it had been modified to run at a single speed of Mach 1.5, for which Miles Aircraft made a special perspex working section of approximately 12in. diameter through which shock waves could be seen and photographed. Although drag measurements could be made on this model in the tunnel, Professor Hilton, who was in charge of these tunnels, considered that the measurements should only be used as an indication, as there was no accurate knowledge of what tunnel corrections, or what effect, if any, Reynolds Number would make. It is unlikely that this model will have been destroyed, but its present whereabouts are unknown.

Model No. 9: To determine the aerodynamic loading of the undercarriage doors because they might, in fact, remain open at very high speeds during take-off and climb (optimum climbing speed approx. 560mph) a model of the fuselage was made to a scale of approximately 1:6.154, principally from softwood with accurately-hinged undercarriage doors.

Model No. 10: A model of the cabin to scale 1:6.154 with various interchangeable attachments, including part of the fuselage, various fabric sleeves, etc., to optimize the stability and provide sufficient drag to reduce the cabin to a reasonable speed to enable the pilot to bale out safely if the cabin had to be jettisoned from the aircraft.

Model No. 11: The RAE then suggested carrying out a set of tests in their high-speed windtunnel, but the Jabroc wing and tail were just not stiff or strong enough to withstand the very much higher loading involved in the much higher wind-speeds. Therefore, solid steel wing and tailplane sections were essential, but keeping the original aluminium alloy fuselage. The wing, etc., were to be machined from a solid billet of steel. This would have to be made from a single sheet of material at least one inch thick, and it was thought that a new, recently-rolled steel billet would tend to deform when machined to such thin sections as the wing needed. An old steel sheet was therefore thought essential. A suitable old sheet was located somewhere in the north of England, and it was thought that in fact it was a piece of an old, scrapped battleship. When the Experimental Department came to machine this steel plate, they thought it must have been at least high-grade armour-plate. The Experimental Department modified a standard shaping machine to produce these wing and tail sections on the basis that all the surfaces were, in fact, a fraction of a perfect cylindrical shape, and the whole process became fully-automatic, but owing to the hardness of the steel and the quantity to be removed, it proved to be a very long job. All sections were finally hand-finished, and after assembly the model was dispatched to the RAE. This model is usually on display at the Berkshire Museum of Aviation, Woodley, Berkshire.

Model No. 12: A mahogany model made approximately to scale 1:24, approximately 13½in. span, painted to represent the finished aircraft, was kept on a stand for demonstration purposes. This completes the list of models made by Miles Aircraft themselves.

Presumably, the NPL made a 7½% bi-convex wing and tested it in their subsonic tunnel, and another 7½% bi-convex wing tested in their supersonic tunnel, the results reported in Aero 2522 of May 1944.

Two views of Model No. 11 at the Berkshire Museum of Aviation, Woodley, Berkshire. They show that the model had flaps and an all-moving tailplane with inboard movable 'notches'.

Model No. 13: The RAE also presumably made a one-quarter-scale model of the E.24/43 wing for test in their No. 2 11½ft windtunnel, with the results being reported in Aero 2044 of June, 1945.

Model No. 14: And finally – Vickers made up to seven quarter-scale rocket-propelled drop models, some of which were dropped without the wings due to rocket development problems. Only the seventh worked properly and made a successful supersonic flight, but the device for automatically ending its flight after about two minutes failed, and the model glided on for a further 80 miles or more, and is now resting at the bottom of the Atlantic Ocean.

REFERENCES

Hilton: May 1944, Aero 2522. Subsonic & Supersonic Tests on a 7½% Biconvex Aerofoil, F.M.694.

Winter & Morgan: July 1944, Aero 1959. Wind Tunnel Tests on the Miles E.24/43 – Part 1.

Hilton & Pruden: February 1945, A.R.C. 7277 & 7703 (revised). Subsonic & Supersonic High-Speed Tunnel Tests of a Faired Double Wedge Aerofoil.

Bancroft: April/August 1945, Various Windtunnel Tests.

Levacic, Marshall & Young: June 1945, Aero 2044. No. 2 11½ft. Wind Tunnel Tests on ¼-scale Model Wing of the Miles E.24/43 Aircraft.

Hutton & Gamble: July 1945, Aero 2057. High-Speed Wind Tunnel Tests on an Aircraft Designed for Supersonic Speeds (Miles E.24/43).

Bancroft: September 1945, The Miles E.24/43. Part I, Miles Report No. 52/0.

Bancroft: February 1946, The Miles E.24/43. Part II, Miles Report No. 52/0a.

HMSO: R & M No. 2835. Flight Trials of a Rocket-Propelled Transonic Research Model: the RAE – Vickers Rocket Model.

Chronology of relevant events

1936	
March	Power Jets Ltd formed by Frank Whittle and partners.

1941	
15 May	First flight of the Gloster/Whittle E.28/39, Britain's first jet-propelled aircraft, flown by P.E.G. Sayer.
2 October	Heini Dittmar, a test pilot for the German Research Institute for Glider Flying at Darmstadt, breaks the 1,000km/h (621mph) barrier in the Messerschmitt 163A third prototype designed by Dr Alexander Lippisch.

1942	
5 January	Eric Brown visits the RAE at Farnborough to test the Miles M.20 fighter and assess it as a possible naval combat aircraft. His report expresses the view that the M.20, although surprisingly nippy in performance, could not match the Wildcat, Hurricane or Spitfire. However he felt that 'the M.20 was indeed a brilliant concept and typical of the genius of the Miles team'.
22 November	Sir Stafford Cripps appointed Minister of Aircraft Production.

1943	
4 May	First Supersonic Committee meeting at MAP. It considers an intelligence report that the Germans were developing high-speed aircraft capable of 1,000mph. This actually should have been 1,000km/h (621mph), although no one seems to have queried it.
4 June	Second Supersonic Committee meeting; the only record available is a selection of the minutes considered at the third meeting.

1943

July (?)

Extract from MOST SECRET document prepared by the Committees and Commissions: Special Projects Development Panel, entitled 'Planning for Jet-Propelled Gas Turbine Aircraft':

Athodyds
The possibility of very high and conceivably supersonic speeds by the use of aero-thermodynamic ducts, referred to as athodyds, has recently been appreciated. The possibility of achievement of such speeds is sufficiently great to warrant an intensive experimental effort. Work with which the RAE is associated has begun at Power Jets Ltd. It is early to say what additional facilities will be required on the laboratory side, but it is certain that some extra provision will have to be made.

Full-Scale Experiment
We shall need capacity for the modification of existing aircraft to do full-scale experiments with high-speed devices. Not only will it be necessary to do experiments in the air with athodyds, but the possibilities of ammonia injection must also be tried as as a means of obtaining the very high speeds necessary for experimenting adequately with the athodyds. This work will need the services of a test pilot of unusual accomplishment.

Very High-Speed Aircraft
It is also necessary to investigate with RAE and NPL the aerodynamic design of aircraft suitable for travelling up to supersonic speeds … It is considered that the help of an enthusiastic constructor like Mr Miles should be enlisted.

6 July

Third meeting of the Supersonic Committee. The Chairman, Ben Lockspeiser, explained that the work on supersonic flight 'had arisen from prisoner of war reports in which it was stated that the Germans had aircraft of this type in flight … Wg Cdr Whittle asked whether some recent PRU photographs, apparently of jet-propelled aircraft on German airfields, had been examined. It was agreed that these photographs should be obtained'.

Mr A.R. Howell introduced RAE report T.N. Eng. 159 and 'stated that for the higher speeds athodyds [simple jet engines consisting essentially of a tube, later known as ram jets] rather than rocket propulsion was the more efficient'. Ram jets would, however, only come into their own when very high speeds had been achieved.

It was confirmed that: 'The overall design of a supersonic aircraft should be considered, as had been agreed at the previous meeting'.

10 August Fourth meeting of the Supersonic Committee. 'The RAE and NPL representatives laid on the table General Arrangement sketches of tentatively proposed layouts. These were monoplanes somewhat similar in appearance, the RAE having wing ducts and the fuel in the body while the NPL one had a fuselage duct and wing tanks.'

18 August Details of the minutes of the fourth meeting sent by the US Embassy to the Director of Aeronautical Research, NACA.

14 September Fifth meeting of the Supersonic Committee discussed 'the potentialities of a gas turbine engine with a fan working in a duct containing propulsive burners ... The Committee unanimously agreed that this is a most promising type of engine for high subsonic and supersonic speeds and that such an engine should be made and tested in flight on high priority.'

25 September Loose minute containing notes of a meeting on future gas turbine engines and aeroplanes held on 25 September:

'(2) To order from (say) Phillips and Powis a very high- speed experimental aeroplane in parallel with which Power Jets would design a supercharged duct fuel burning turbine engine, adapted from one of their current types.'

29 September Memorandum from Air Marshal Ralph Sorley to Norbert Rowe (through Dr Roxbee Cox): 'I agree that it is necessary for us to design and build for trial the most advanced form of aircraft to use the type of engine described in Minute 1. The greatest benefit we can obtain from such an aircraft will be achieved by building it quickly in order to get some practical answers on this high speed problem. Therefore, I think that we must not complicate it by considering operational features which are certain to delay the project. We must regard this as a research and development item. Consequently I would be prepared to offer this to Miles who is probably the best man to produce the article quickly.'

1943

5 October	Phillips and Powis Aircraft Ltd changes name to Miles Aircraft Ltd.
8 October	Letter from Air Marshal Ralph Sorley to F.G. Miles confirming that the Ministry of Aircraft Production was rejecting the projected Miles M.26L X.11 transport aeroplane. To lessen the blow Sorley added that he would 'like to discuss at an early date some work I have in mind for you which will require to be dealt with quickly. I know that DTD is getting into touch with you almost at once and I shall be happy to discuss the matter with you in due course.'
9 October	Directorate of Technical Development meeting at the Ministry of Aircraft Production, with Dr H.M. Garner, Norbert Rowe, Dr Roxbee Cox, F.G. Miles and Gp Capt Frank Whittle. Notes on the meeting report that 'The purpose of the meeting was to initiate action on a very high-speed experimental aeroplane. Phillips & Powis were to make the aeroplane which was to be powered with a W.2/700 with No. 4 augmenter (*sic*) and bypass heating. Rough dimensions for the power unit and duct sizes were given to Miles.'
	The all-up weight should be around 5,000–6,000lb; target speed 1,000mph; fuel for climb to 40,000ft and half an hour at 700mph; target date 9 months hence. It was to be a monoplane with a large, wholly moving, tailplane. Skids instead of an undercarriage were to be considered.
12 October	Sixth meeting of the Supersonic Committee. No mention of the Miles E.24/43.
17 October (Sunday)	Visit of Miles team, consisting of Lionel 'Toby' Heal (Chief Designer), Dennis Bancroft (Chief Aerodynamicist) and W.B. Barnes (Chief Draughtsman on the M52), to Power Jets at Whetstone and Brownsover Hall. Received by Gp Capt Frank Whittle, Wg Cdr George Lees, Leslie Cheshire, Julian Hodge and FO W.E.P. Johnson. Notes on the meeting were supplied by Johnson. At Whetstone the Miles team were shown various engines and saw a 700 running. At Brownsover it was agreed that Miles should design 'up to the limit of present knowledge and experience, leaving further performance to ad hoc development, while Power Jets were to provide power for the full performance required by MAP'.

1943

'Layouts of aircraft were then discussed, FW putting in a word for biplane or multiplane arrangements. The usual round of specific problems were mentioned, e.g. pilot accommodation, tankage, and undercarriage stowage. Automatic instrument observation is accepted and we quoted 25/30lb as the Observer weight (they had thought 15lb). FW considered the tricycle layout to be desirable.

We were asked about weights and gave the following for guidance: W.2/700, 850–900lb; Augmenter 300lb. Ducting – depends on layout; extra combustion 100lb.

The matter of gearboxes was discussed; the front mounting point probably being 'out' and the storage space and fairing in the entry duct being a significant problem, it is proposed to try a G.E.C. gearbox complete on the 700, so as to pack all aircraft auxiliaries as well as engine auxiliaries, as near the main axis as possible with a view to fitting a nose fairing.

The Miles Aircraft project of using wing-tank structure was viewed somewhat suspiciously, but an annular tank seemed to be common ground.

Mr Heal requested an installation or G.A. of W.2/700.

Dennis Bancroft recorded that 'Power Jets estimate that thrust at 1,000mph at 36,000ft was 5,000lb; they expect an increase of 25% next year'.

23 October Preliminary note on Miles-Power Jets very high-speed aircraft by Gp Capt Frank Whittle (see Appendix 1).

29 October Memorandum from Dr Roxbee Cox to Norbert Rowe. '… I have just been to Phillips and Powis at their request, and saw their projects. They are going into more detail on the most conventional of them, and it is my view that we might give them another week and then have a solid sort of meeting at which the many points which I gather they will wish to raise can be discussed.

They showed me an Agenda which covered such matters as labour requirements, passes to aerodromes and factories, load factors, stiffness criteria, aileron reversal, tail loading, aerodynamics data, shape of wing tips, together with a large number of engine installation problems. My suggestion would be to attempt to clear as many of these at as small a meeting as possible.'

He suggests those at the meeting should be himself and Norbert Rowe, Dr H.M. Garner, Dr Pugsley, Ronald Smelt (head of the High-Speed section of the Aerodynamics Department, RAE), Gp Capt Frank Whittle (who might have had to send a substitute because he was in hospital), Leslie Cheshire (Power Jets), and ADSP(F) to give a pilot's view.

'Two points raised by Miles with me were:

(a) Are we trying to get such information as there may be on supersonic flight from Italy (I am referring this to DSR)?

(b) Miles wants the Falcon at present at the RAE back at Reading as quickly as possible. I understand you have agreed to its going there, but he is in a hurry to do a particular experiment.'

6 November (Saturday)   Norbert Rowe (DTD) visits Miles at Woodley with other MAP and Power Jets personnel. He proposes to Air Marshal Sorley (CRD) the placing of a contract for two prototypes and parts for a third.

8 November   Letter from George Miles to Norbert Rowe headed 'Gyrone, (Whittle's name for a turbojet) Project' and enclosing drawings and other data on the ultra high-speed project, as promised to Rowe on his visit to Woodley on 6 November. 'The description of the aircraft is intentionally brief since we felt that it was the opinion of all concerned that the design should be left fairly open at this stage'. The letter goes on to stress that the priority allocated to the project would affect the acquisition of scarce materials, such as high grade aluminium alloys and the extra staff which would be required. As agreed Miles would go ahead with two aircraft to begin with and obtain material for at least three machines. The aim would be to complete the first aircraft within one year.

Full-scale flight tests would be carried out and a request was made for the loan of a Mustang or Spitfire. Subsonic tests would be carried out in the Miles wind tunnel as soon as it was finished; Dennis Bancroft would be discussing the problem of supersonic tests with RAE and NPL during the week.

9 November Seventh meeting of the Supersonic Committee. After discussion about rocket models and wind tunnel tests, Norbert Rowe 'remarked that it was appropriate here to mention the Miles high-speed aircraft which had been proposed. A brief description of the aircraft was then given'.

November Visit of Miles design team to the Aeronautical Department of the National Physical Laboratory (NPL), Teddington, to meet Dr Ernest Relf and Dr Hilton.

November Miles team visit Dr J.W. Maccoll at the Armament Research Department (ARD) at Fort Halstead, to discuss high-speed ballistics.

11 November Memorandum from Norbert Rowe to Air Marshal Ralph Sorley, generally approving the designs enclosed with George Miles letter. He feels that 'the firm has shown, by the way they have tackled the initial stages, that we could safely entrust this project to them' and asks for Sorley's agreement to the placing of the contract for two prototypes and parts for a third and 'concurrence in the high priority Miles asks for'.

12 November Meeting at RAE with full Miles team (Bancroft, Barnes, Brown, Heal, George Miles and Wilkinson) and A.R. Collar, G.P. Douglas, R. Graham, A.R. Howell, S.R. Smelt, D. Williams from RAE. Detailed discussion of the designs for the fuselage, wings, controls and cabin. The NPL were making HST tests of the wing section and RAE agreed to make HST tests of a complete model, probably one-quarter scale, which would be made at RAE. The Miles team were informed that RAE had no supersonic wind tunnels and no method of measuring transonic drag. A Falcon at RAE would be allotted to Miles for modification to the wing shape. A false nose and tail would be built on to the wing to give the bi-convex section, and flight tests would be made. They agreed to watch the question of aileron control closely.

1943

15 November	Letter from Air Marshal Ralph Sorley to Norbert Rowe, agreeing to the placing of the contract but qualifying degree of priority given to the project.
17 November	Memorandum from Norbert Rowe to DD/RDT instructing him to place the contract with Miles as a matter of urgency. An early meeting was also to be arranged to settle priorities.
17 November	Letter from Norbert Rowe to F.G. Miles confirming the decision to place a contract 'for the experimental project'. RAE to come up with the choice of engine as quickly as possible. Enclosed, a form relating to the Official Secrets Act to be signed.
26 November	Letter from Norbert Rowe to J.E. Serby saying that he is holding on to the requisition for the three aircraft (one to be supplied in component parts only) because RAE have concluded the layout of the aircraft as envisaged will not achieve 600mph at 40,000ft. He will hold on to the requisition until he knows the results of a meeting between Dr H.M. Garner (the Deputy Director of Scientific Research) and F.G. Miles about a possible redesign to reduce wing drag.
30 November	Loose minute from J.E. Serby to Norbert Rowe confirming that a meeting had taken place between Dr Garner and himself and F.G. Miles and his designer. Miles did not refute RAE estimates of 570mph at 40,000. After discussion of multi-engined machines Miles agreed to design and build two sets of wings to reduce the aspect ratio. The minute includes this important paragraph: 'We discussed ailerons and tail control, and agreed that as life was short and time was fleeting the more important of these to develop ahead of his actual aeroplane was the all moving tail. It will be necessary for him to design and prove such a mechanism on an orthodox aeroplane, probably a Spitfire, before he fits it on his high-speed aircraft.'
1 December	Letter from Dr Garner to F.G. Miles confirming the details of the discussion but querying whether there would be any purpose in carrying out aileron tests on a Spitfire because of the great difference between the wings of the project and the Spitfire.

3 December Letter from Dr Roxbee Cox sent to Leslie Cheshire at Power Jets suggesting a meeting with Dr J.W. Maccoll of the Armament Research Department – the Ordnance Board's aerodynamic expert – to discuss high-speed ballistics.

Telephone conversation between Ronald Smelt of the Aerodynamics Department, RAE, and Leslie Cheshire, Power Jets (at the request of Dr Roxbee Cox), concerning the drag estimations and insufficient power for the engine for the M.52. Leslie Cheshire confirmed that 'we could now increase the thrust available considerably above the figure which had been previously given, which would go a long way to reducing the deficiency'. A visit arranged for Cheshire and, hopefully, Frank Whittle to the RAE.

13 December Contract for E.24/43 placed with Miles Aircraft (actually dated 29 December).

14 December Eighth meeting of the Supersonic Committee. Dr Garner summarised the problems on the performance of the aircraft and what was being done to provide higher performance. Ronald Smelt (RAE) mentioned that Power Jets 'was now able to offer approximately twice the thrust by using temperatures up to 1500° and other modifications'. When Dr Roxbee Cox queried the accuracy of the steep increase in the curve of drag against Mach No., Ronald Smelt said the results were reasonably reliable, as far as Mach=0.9 but evidence above that 'was flimsy, owing to the interference drag effect being almost unknown'. In answer to a question from Dr Griffith, Dr Roxbee Cox said that Power Jets had originally designed for a variable outlet duct but had dropped it because their calculations suggested that it was not necessary. A.R. Howell (RAE, later Power Jets) agreed to discuss the matter with Frank Whittle. Other subjects discussed included whether the wings should be subsonic or supersonic, wind tunnel tests, the use of a Falcon for tests at subsonic speeds on a supersonic wing, and the allotment of priorities. Dr Roxbee Cox would now take contract action on the engine and DSR would take contract action on the aircraft.

1943

18 December Conference held at NACA to discuss jet propulsion advancements in Britain, with representation from NACA, USAAF, US Navy and eight industrial firms.

19 December Bell Aircraft briefed on the USAAF Wright Field's Engineering Division's internal conceptual study of a proposed near-sonic experimental project, referred to as 'the Mach 0.999 rocket-powered airplane'.

20 December A meeting in Dr Garner's office discussed the wings of the M.52. George Miles pointed out 'that the chief difficulty in thinning the wing lay in the attachment to the fuselage … a small wing area was necessary to get very thin wings'. A Falcon should be fitted out with a new wing of thickness/chord 7.5%; it would take about three months to provide a new fuel system. A Spitfire was preferred to a Mustang for tests of the all-moving tail.

28 December A loose minute from J.E. Serby to Norbert Rowe and Air Marshal Ralph Sorley expresses alarm at the volume of work Miles has 'on his plate'. A letter had been sent to Miles with the following list:

1   Monitor [M.33 – a twin-engined monoplane].

2   M.38.

3   Martinet with drone [trial installation just about to be ordered on two aeroplanes. In 1943 work commenced on the modification of the Martinet to specification Q.10/43. This called for a ground operated radio controlled pilotless version of the M.26 Martinet TT Mk 1 which later became known as the M.50 Queen Martinet].

4   Martinet and Master.

5   Two prototypes of E.24/43. Development work planned to aid this: (a) Design of all moving electrically controlled tailplane to be tested first on Spitfire. (b) Fitting of sonic speed wing profile on Falcon to check characteristics of such sections in flight.

6   M.18.

7   M.39 [the tandem wing Libellula project].

1944

3 January

A letter from F.G. Miles to J.E. Serby, in reply to the letter of 28 December, states that all the items listed are 'irrelevant to this narrative' except item 5. The amount of time on this depends largely on the priority given to the work. It also suggests a visit from Serby to discuss matters.

3 January

Julian Hodge of Power Jets reports on the minutes of the eighth meeting of the Supersonic Committee. He criticises the RAE performance estimates and says that Dr J.W. Maccoll, 'the only person who could be of any great help in this respect', believes the supersonic drag estimates used by the RAE, 'especially that relating to scale effect, is very badly wrong'.

He also points out 'a misapprehension about the ultimate wing thickness to be aimed at' and many other inaccuracies in the information presented to the committee.

3 January

Memorandum from Dr H.M. Garner (through Ben Lockspeiser and J.E. Serby) to Norbert Rowe lists 'some change in the proposals laid down in my letter of 1st December as a result of discussions at the Supersonic Committee on 14 December 1943 and with Miles Aircraft on 20 December 1943. The committee decided that as for wings of 7½% thick or less the behaviour at low speeds was according to wind-tunnel tests, hardly affected by the shape of the section and in view of the advantage of a sharp leading edge at high speeds a wing with this feature was desirable. This brings back the importance of tests of wings on the Falcon and these are being arranged. Tests on all-moving power-operated tailplane on the Spitfire are also being arranged.'

In an old wartime works file George Miles, referring to a telephone conversation with the MAP, questions the limited amount of space in the rear fuselage of the Spitfire in which to install power-operated controls for the all-moving tailplane. He goes on to say that it would not be insurmountable.

11 January — Memorandum from Ben Lockspeiser to Dr Roxbee Cox explaining that he had 'tried to seek out the best brains in the country for the Supersonic Committee … where firms are engaged on work for the Committee, their work should be presented through the Directorate concerned'. '*Should the Committee wish to question the detail of this work and discuss it with any particular member of the firm, I should invite the person concerned to attend a meeting for the purpose*'. Group Captain Whittle was, unfortunately, ill.

12 January — Gloster Meteor with the Whittle Welland engines (i.e. production version of the W.2B) makes its maiden flight at Farnborough. Shortly afterwards Eric Brown flies Meteor EE214/G, becoming the first naval pilot to fly a jet aircraft.

15 January — Letter from Dr Roxbee Cox to Wing Commander George Lees, Whittle's deputy, asking for the performance and maximum thrust figures (a) for the W.2/700 alone; (b) for the W.2/700 plus ducted fan; (c) for the W.2/700 plus ducted fan and afterburning.

15 January — Memorandum from Norbert Rowe to Director of Aircraft Production, requesting priority for material for the three prototypes.

17 January — Eric Brown joins Aerodynamics Flight at RAE Farnborough.

19 January — Statement of Estimated Performance of W.2/700 with No. 4 Design Thrust Augmentor in M.52 prepared by Power Jets. A report, to be issued shortly, would deal with methods of obtaining increased output at high speeds at altitude, including use of W.2/800 instead of W.2/700.

4 February — Letter from Dr H.M. Garner to F.G. Miles asking for Miles proposals for the E.24/43 and for the fitting of a thin wing to the Falcon, after a meeting with RAE and NPL arranged for 10 February.

Garner confirms that they 'propose to order two complete aircraft of the E.24/43 type with parts for a third'. He goes on to make the point 'if your present idea of constructing the wing 7.5% thick at the root and tapering to 4% at the tip, and building up the wing to 10% by means of plasters for the first flight is adhered to, there would only be one design of metal wings. This would save a lot of time, as compared with the original proposal to produce two designs'.

8 February

Memorandum from Edward Sara (ADMP.5) to Norbert Rowe confirming that 'every attention to the supply of materials for these three prototype aircraft' was to be given and any problems reported.

2–3 March

In America, first meeting of the High-Speed Panel at Langley Memorial Aeronautical Laboratory, Virginia. It was agreed that research would focus on the conventional plane and special jet categories; three types of aeroplanes were discussed: subsonic propeller, jet-propelled and supersonic.

7 March

Meeting held at the Ministry of Aircraft Production to discuss the preliminary draft specification for the E.24/43. Present at the meeting were Dr H.M. Garner (Chairman); J.E. Serby; F.G. Miles, D.L. Brown, L.C. Heal, H.S. Wilkinson, D. Bancroft, W.B. Barnes from Miles Aircraft; A.F. Walsh (RTO); R.C. McLeod and L.J. Cheshire from Power Jets; R. Smelt, P.E. Montagnon from RAE; E.F. Relf from NPL; and five other civil servants.

The draft specification was subjected to detailed analysis, clause by clause. At the end of the meeting it was agreed that Miles Aircraft 'should attempt to obtain, on loan, a test pilot of suitable dimensions for the aircraft for the period of the initial flight tests if undertaken by the firm'.

The Chairman emphasised that no departure from this specification was to be made unless 'there were serious reasons in the light of our accumulating knowledge for so doing'. Any such departure must be approved by MAP Headquarters.

14 March

Eleventh meeting of the Supersonic Committee. Dr H.M. Garner reported that the specification for the E.24/43 had been discussed at the meeting on 7 March and the design should not now change appreciably. The Chairman had spoken to F.G. Miles and 'had been impressed by the firm's enthusiasm, and felt that they were making extremely good progress'.

18 March

Letter from L.J. Cheshire of Power Jets to Lionel Heal of Miles Aircraft Ltd, enclosing details of the estimated performance of the M.52: (a) with W.2/700 and No. 4 design Thrust Augmentor and (b) with W.2/700 alone.

1944

Power Jets estimate that it would take about 120 gallons of fuel plus 20 gallons take-off allowance for the aircraft to get to 60,000ft. They confirm the figures for other fuel consumptions: '10 gallons for the dive to 36,000ft and 85 gallons for 5 minutes at 1,000mph at 36,000ft. It is difficult to say how long the remaining 55 gallons will last, but this quantity of fuel should be sufficient for at least half an hour's low speed running while losing altitude or more than this with the bypass heating turned off.' The top speed of the aircraft at ground level worked out at about 645mph, entirely dependent on the Mach No. at which the compressibility effect becomes serious; this is 'fairly certainly not an appreciable overestimate'. With only the W.2/700 the top speed at ground level should be about 415mph and the ceiling about 35,000ft.

April

Two W.2/700 engines installed in a Meteor and test flown.

11 April

Twelfth meeting of the Supersonic Committee. Dr Roxbee Cox stated that only a few months' work was required on the W.2/700 with No. 4 Augmentor and if the aircraft was not built quickly other aircraft would be built which would compete in speed.

17 April

Memorandum from R.N. Liptrot to P.S.15 and C.23 (c) enclosing an authorisation for an additional prototype E.24/43 and asking for financial approval for a further £30,000.

27 April

Sqn Ldr Tony Martindale (RAE) achieves M=0.92 in Spitfire PR X1. The Spitfire had been stripped of all operational equipment so that it was well below its normal weight. Even so it required Martindale, a powerful six-footer, to pull 100lb on the control column to recover from the dive. At that point the over-speeding propeller became detached, with its reduction gear. 'Marty' blacked out but managed to land the Spitfire whose straight wing had acquired a slightly swept back look; it was a write-off.

28 April

Power Jets (R & D) Ltd formally established as a government-owned company with Dr Roxbee Cox as Chairman and Managing Director. Included in the new company were all scientists in the Engine Experimental Department of the RAE who were working on gas turbines with the Whittle team. Whittle later became Chief Technical Adviser to the Board.

3 May — Meeting at the RAE to discuss low-speed tunnel test results. Present: Messrs Squire (Chairman), Gates, Hills, Winter, Anscombe, Flt Lt Mair and Miss Fougère from the Aero Dept, RAE; Messrs Heal, Bancroft, Wilkinson and Capley from Miles Aircraft Ltd.

8 May — Memorandum for the attention of Dr H.M. Garner from Dr G.P. Douglas, for the Director, RAE, suggesting modifications to the design following the meeting on 3 May. It was also suggested that a half-scale complete wooden model would be more convenient for the low-speed model tests.

9 May — Thirteenth meeting of the Supersonic Committee. Problems caused by the increase in weight discussed. Dr H.M. Garner reported that the weight of the aircraft had increased from 5,140lb normal and 6,500lb overload to 7,754lb normal and 8,564lb overload. Part of the increase was due to the increased fuel weight (70 gallons more) and part due to the increased engine weight, quoted as 1,350lb but now 1,920lb.

13 June — Fourteenth meeting of the Supersonic Committee. Dr H.M. Garner stated that performance figures had been requested at the new weights. Ronald Smelt confirmed that these had been completed; the ceiling was now about 50,000ft and not 60,000ft as originally calculated; this was based on Miles' weight estimates. After some discussion about the bi-convex wing Ronald Smelt said he calculated the top speed would now be 630mph at 36,000ft. Owing to the decreased ceiling it was now doubtful whether the aircraft would reach supersonic speeds in a dive.

'Sir Melvill-Jones asked, in view of the fact that British and American jet-propelled aircraft, described by Dr Griffith and Mr Smelt, were reaching very high speed, whether the E.24/43 should be proceeded with.'

The possibility of changing the engine, making a larger aircraft and the use of rockets of the bi-fuel type to boost the thrust were all considered. The weight increase was thought to be the decisive factor.

The Chairman, Ben Lockspeiser, asked for 'a general appreciation of the design of aeroplane capable of supersonic flight [to] be prepared, all designs of proposed engines being considered, and suggested that the relative suitabilities of bi-convex and normal wings be investigated.

Further the performance of the E.24/43 should be examined with engines which will be available and can be installed without serious modification.'

16 June

Notes by Leslie Cheshire (Power Jets) of a meeting at Whetstone between Dr Maccoll, Dr Haworth and Mr Illingworth of the Armament Research Department, Dennis Bancroft and Walter Capley of Miles Aircraft Ltd and Leslie Cheshire, Julian Hodge and A.G. Smith of Power Jets.

It was agreed that the unreliable and excessive drag estimates prepared by Ronald Smelt were very different from the estimates prepared by Dr Maccoll, those obtained in the NPL wind tunnel, those by A.G. Smith from the small model or Miles Aircraft estimate. 'There was general agreement that the wing and tail drag was very near to 2,000lb, giving a total drag for the aircraft of 6,000lb. Based on the present design, the total thrust will be slightly over 4,000lb at 36,000ft at full forward speed, so that on this basis, level flight at M=1.5 will not be obtained.' Power Jets asked if the area through the tail spar could be increased: Walter Capley later phoned to say the diameter could be increased by 3 inches, which would be a great help. It was finally agreed that Miles would finalise the airframe and Power Jets would carry on with the existing engine-augmentor design but would consider: (a) methods of obtaining thrust by means of a new design of augmentor blades and combustion; (b) review the whole problem from the power plant standpoint which might involve some modification to the rear end of the aircraft and (c) consider the question of drag reduction. Any proposals which involved important structural alterations to the aircraft would be put to Miles Aircraft. Walter Capley pointed out that if a pilot had to be carried the overall diameter could not be reduced appreciably; the most promising line in drag reduction was to increase the fineness of the nose. Dr Maccoll, who had not based his estimates on the latest improved shape, undertook to provide a new estimate within two weeks. Miles, in collaboration with Power Jets, would prepare a set of aircraft performance figures as the authoritative estimates when they received Dr Maccoll's revised estimates.

28 June	Notes by G. White of the visit of Julian Hodge, Messrs Leach and White of Power Jets to Miles Aircraft to discuss outstanding points on the W.2/700M and the M52:

1. Power Jets suggestion to put the oil tank on the top of the gear box was not possible because the space is already taken up with control mechanisms. Miles suggested it could be built into the aircraft structure just aft of the secondary inlet on the port side of the top dead centre line.

2. Miles suggested that the oil pipe to the augmentor bearings should be heated with hot air.

3. Miles asked if it was possible to arrange pick-up points between the joint flange and the outlet flange on the turbine end of the lower casing.

4. Miles supplied drawings for their suggested position of the fuel and igniter connections to athodyd.

5. Miles suggested the annular gap at the end of the fuselage between skin and jet pipe should be reduced and this was agreed.

6. Power Jets would supply the connection between the anemometer control and athodyd fuel control pilot valve.

7. Miles could not promise any increase in the inner diameter of the tailplane frames to allow more room for the rear attachment anchorage. They pointed out the axial position of these frames in their latest drawing was not final.

8. Miles supplied more detailed information on the inside of the fuselage and particulars of the rear end profile. Power Jets promised to supply a drawing giving all the leading dimensions of the W.2/700M, No. 4 Augmentor and athodyd and a more detailed weight analysis.

27 July	Meeting at Reading with Dr H.M. Garner, H.F. Vessey and Miles Aircraft representatives. The considerable growth in weight since the original proposals, and ways in which reductions could be made, was discussed. A rigid weight control would be applied and it was hoped to save weight

in the detail design and in the weight involved in jettisoning the cabin. Dr Garner pointed out that even with this reduction in weight, there would be an appreciable deterioration in performance in comparison with the original estimates and asked that Miles should re-estimate the take-off climb and landing conditions – in particular a re-assessment of the fuel required to climb to altitude.

Dr Garner stated that a strength test on a complete airframe (which Miles believed would be completed long before October) could be undertaken by RAE after October of this year. Miles also wished to make strength tests on a wing and tailplane; they had the necessary equipment.

Almost two years later the two officers of the US Air Technical Section, Majors E.N. Hall and Kent Parrot, who visited Woodley on 8 July 1946, reported: 'The firm now has all jigging and tooling completed and about 90% of all airframe components fabricated, but not assembled for Model No. 2. Model No. 1 was completed and destroyed in a series of satisfactory static tests [presumably at the RAE]'.

Dr Garner also agreed to Miles continuing work on a power system capable of operating the tailplane with a view to installation in a Spitfire for the moveable tailplane investigation, subject to RAE agreement that their design was promising. Suitable radio equipment was also considered.

This confirms that Miles was proceeding with the moveable tailplane investigation on the Spitfire.

27 July First Meteor Is, powered by Rolls-Royce Wellands (production version of the W.2B), begin operations against V.1 flying bombs.

4 August Eric Brown receives note from W.S. Farren, Director of RAE, asking him 'to start taking a close interest in the supersonic research programme'.

4 August Memorandum from Dr H.M. Garner to J.E. Serby, replying to a memorandum of 2 August: 'We had a long discussion ... and decided to go ahead with the supersonic wings but to have wings with rounded leading edges as a second string. Miles and RAE are to discuss the latter....'

8 August

At the fifteenth meeting of the Supersonic Committee, Ronald Smelt said Aero Tech Note No. 1470, compiled by C.M. Fougère of RAE, based on the latest wind tunnel tests, suggested that a higher Mach No. (1.06) in the dive would be obtainable with conventional wings rather than bi-convex wings (1.03). The drag of the fuselage was much higher than anticipated – an estimated value of CD max of 0.15 against 0.08. Dr Maccoll said his calculations indicated the drag of the present fuselage was much higher than the previous design, partly due to the bad design aft of the lip of the intake but mainly due to the sudden narrowing of the fuselage at the rear – a drag of 4,000lb at Mach=1.5; a drag of 3,000lb could be achieved under the same conditions. A meeting was to be held with Miles on the following day to discuss the fuselage shape.

In answer to doubts about the drag for the bi-convex wing the Chairman, Ben Lockspeiser, said he had decided the bi-convex wing should have first priority because one of the main objects of the experiment was to find out about supersonic wings; there was also the possibility of a 50% increase in engine power which would considerably reduce the adverse margin of thrust required for level flight. The work on a conventional wing would go ahead on a lower priority.

11 August

'Gillette' Falcon, modified to be the M.52E Falcon Six, makes its first flight with the M.52 type bi-convex wing, but with straight leading/trailing edges instead of the slightly curved edges. It retained its standard tailplane, and was flown by Miles test pilot, Flt Lt Hugh Kennedy.

26 August

Full specification (dated 14.8.44), incorporating the actual work already done by Miles since October 1943, issued to Miles Aircraft Ltd.

6 September

General overall layout for the M.52 completed.

12 September

At the sixteenth meeting of the Supersonic Committee it was announced that the Falcon with bi-convex wings had flown successfully. It was believed the stalling speed would be lower than originally expected; the large drag increase with incidence was evident in the take-off; the lateral control was stated to be exceptionally good.

1944

A note from Dr Maccoll stated that at a meeting with Miles on 9 August several designs of fuselage had been considered and Miles had produced modified designs showing a drag reduction of around 10%.

The Chairman (Ben Lockspeiser) stated that the aircraft should be built as at present envisaged to avoid delay with the flight tests.

Autumn

MAP arranges a visit to Miles Aircraft by Americans representing USAAF, NACA and Bell Aircraft Corporation. They take away general arrangement drawings of the M.52.

10 October

Seventeenth meeting of the Supersonic Committee. Work was proceeding on the aircraft but only 16 draughtsmen were employed on the project. It was agreed to allocate 32 draughtsmen to the aircraft so that the first flight tests should be made in the fine weather of May/June instead of October. Flight tests on the Falcon were proceeding. Mr Smelt 'had recommended that flight tests be made on a standard Falcon for comparative purposes. An attempt was being made to obtain a suitable aircraft'. Power Jets had proposed using an axial engine – the Q-1.

19 October

Letter to Wg Cdr Wilson, Experimental Flight Dept, RAE, from Dr Garner, asking him to keep in touch with Miles and RDQ(F) to ensure that the pilot's instruments are positioned to enable the test pilots to make careful and accurate observations.

14 November

At the eighteenth meeting of the Supersonic Committee, Mr Vessey states that the Falcon with the bi-convex wings is now at RAE being fitted with the bi-convex tailplane [with elevator]. If the first flights are successful the aircraft would be returned to Reading. High-speed tunnel tests would be starting soon.

21 November

Flt Lt Hugh Kennedy carries out a twenty-five minute test flight of the Falcon from Farnborough.

12 December

Nineteenth meeting of the Supersonic Committee. The Falcon was now fitted with bi-convex wings and tailplane and flight tests had been made. 'It was now proposed to fit an all-moving bi-convex tail to the Falcon and dispense with proposed tests on a power operated bi-convex tailplane for the Spitfire.' The National Physical Laboratory tunnel had run at supersonic speeds and taken photographs of the shock waves on the model.

1945

1 January	Meteor I, with aperture cut for a flight observer, with Whittle W.2/700 engine with afterburning capability, flown by Eric Brown.
9 January	Twentieth meeting of the Supersonic Committee. Dr Garner was asked to take up the question of supplying more draughtsmen for the project.
15 January	Churchill issues a directive to stop research and development work which would not be operational by mid-1946 (see Appendix 6).
13 February	Twenty-first meeting of the Supersonic Committee. Ronald Smelt (RAE) had produced notes on a rocket-propelled aircraft, small enough to be carried on a Lancaster to about 20,000ft. The pilot's compartment was the same as that on the E.24/43. This could be a good proposal for attaining supersonic flight quickly. R. McKinnon Wood had prepared a drawing of a tri-fuselage aircraft for high supersonic speeds – two of the fuselages containing engines – thus permitting pitot entry.
23 February	A Department of Scientific Research paper, by Dr H.M. Garner, listing the experimental aircraft constructional work which is in hand for research purposes includes this on the Miles E.24/43: 'this aircraft is being built to investigate the problems of flight at speeds exceeding that of sound. The wing section is appropriate to supersonic flight, having sharp leading and trailing edges, and although the machine will not exceed the speed of sound in level flight, it is hoped that it will be possible to do so by diving. The aircraft is a single seater, weighing about 8,000lb and is powered by a jet turbine engine from which additional power is obtained by burning fuel in the jet pipe. The contract SB.27157/C23c was placed on 29.12.43 and the aircraft is expected to be in flight early in 1946.'

13 March — Twenty-second meeting of the Supersonic Committee. It was reported that the Falcon with the bi-convex wing and all-moving tailplane had now been flown successfully. The aircraft was now a designated aircraft with a high priority. The design of an aircraft powered by Power Jets' new engine, which would be available in two years, should proceed. It would be difficult to find an aircraft firm to collaborate with Power Jets because of the shortage of design facilities in the country. Dr Roxbee Cox approved of the twin-engined layout because the weight was distributed along the span and another advantage was the pitot entry as the annular entry was not considered good. It had been agreed that a rocket-propelled aircraft would be the quickest method of obtaining supersonic flight. After discussion about the type of aircraft required Dr Garner suggested, as an interim measure, a rocket should be fitted in the E.24/43; this would require another fuselage. Ben Lockspeiser felt the capsule should be piloted, as experience must be gained of flying at the speeds under consideration. In response to the Churchill directive, the Chairman had drawn a list of items deemed exempt – the very top item on the list is the M.52!

16 March — USAAF launches its formal supersonic aircraft programme by awarding a contract to the Bell Aircraft Corporation for three rocket-powered aircraft, to be built to USAAF specifications, but with technical inputs from NACA (the American equivalent of RAE). The aircraft were designated XS-1 (X = experimental, S = supersonic); the S was eventually deleted.

According to Richard P. Hallion in *Supersonic Flight* 'NACA recommended that the stabilizer itself be adjustable by the pilot while in flight', i.e. adjustable tailplane, controllable elevator, as distinct from the fully controllable powered tailplane planned for the M.52.

April — Miles Gillette Falcon flown by three RAE High-Speed Flight pilots, including Eric Brown.

10 April — Twenty-third meeting of the Supersonic Committee. It was agreed that both the jet-propelled and rocket-propelled aircraft should be proceeded with. Scale models should be used to investigate the transition period with a pilot flying the full-scale rocket-propelled aircraft so that the control characteristics in the transition period near Mach 1.0 could be investigated. The Chairman, Ben Lockspeiser, suggested the Martin-Baker company be approached because they had no work. He would also approach Barnes Wallis of Vickers-Armstrong for assistance in the design of the models.

9 May

Douglas D-558 proposal for six supersonic aircraft approved. Estimated cost £1.64 million; only one supersonic flight achieved, much later, in a 35-degree dive on 29 September 1948.

12 June

(8 May meeting cancelled because it was VE day) Twenty-fourth meeting of the Supersonic Committee. Barnes Wallis joined the committee.

Since the Dambuster Raid in 1943 Wallis, who had been emotionally affected by the number of casualties suffered in that operation, had declared he would never send any airman to his death if he could possibly avoid it. He considered the M.52 a high risk and this no doubt was behind his strong advocacy for using pilotless rocket-powered models in place of the jet-propelled aircraft. At the time Wallis was Assistant Chief Designer, Aviation Section of Vickers, working on rocket-driven drop models. He had a great influence on the other members of the Supersonic Committee and played a major part in the decision to cancel the contract for the M.52.

H.F. Vessey stated the E.24/43 was in trouble and listed problems: the Cm0 was higher than estimated, making the tail loads more difficult to accommodate from the structural aspect; a serious decrease of longitudinal stability with increase of Mach number, commencing at M=0.5. (At the next meeting Vessey reported that the problems 'were not as serious as had first been envisaged'). The RAE had recommended the c.g. should be further forward. A meeting had been arranged on 18 June to discuss the problems.

Ben Lockspeiser, the Chairman, gave a brief history of the E.24/43 and stated that 'as time went on the aircraft had become less and less likely to succeed. Against this he was not sure of the results of the tunnel tests on the E.24/43 as various difficulties had been encountered in interpretation of tunnel tests in the past'.

In view of information from Germany he believed it would 'be desirable to have a large amount of sweepback or sweepforward on the wings of a supersonic aircraft'. The possible advantages and probable effects were discussed. Power Jets were proceeding, slowly, with their improved power plant. Ben Lockspeiser referred to reports that the US Navy had initiated two designs for high-speed research aircraft to operate at supersonic speeds, achieving a Mach number of 1.1 in level flight for about two minutes. Both designs were for conventional low-wing monoplanes with a mixed power plant of jet propulsion engine and rockets which provided an additional thrust of 6,000lb for two minutes. Pitot entries were to be fitted (a pitot form of air intake could prove more efficient at high speed than an annular air intake).

Ben Lockspeiser gave a brief summary of the position on the rocket-propelled aircraft. He had recently been in Germany and had been told that LFA in Brunswick had achieved supersonic speeds with a rocket with wings. Barnes Wallis had been asked to investigate the design of 'such small aircraft'. A large number of bi-fuel rockets was now available in Germany. An Mė 163B, with a Walter rocket giving a thrust of 3,740lb for a period of about eight minutes, was available at RAE and flight tests would proceed as soon as possible. It was agreed that Barnes Wallis should 'in the first instance investigate briefly the possibility of manufacturing and designing small aircraft for the purpose'. He suggested 'that the first shape should be a model of the Miles E.24/43'.

10 July   Twenty-fifth meeting of the Supersonic Committee. The importance of the effect of sweepback at very high speeds was discussed and Dr Griffith asked if 'any attempt was being made to include this feature in service aircraft now being designed'. Norbert Rowe described three new types of service aircraft. In two cases sweepback was being considered. Dr Garner called attention to the low speed difficulties of sweepback or sweepforward and said it would take some time before we have enough knowledge for it to be introduced with reasonable certainty of success. Norbert Rowe agreed the amount of sweepback required would be large. Dr Kurt Tank (the Focke-Wulf designer) had stressed that for any real advantage sweepback of around 45° would be necessary.

H.F. Vessey reported 'that the problems reported at the last meeting were not as serious as had first been envisaged. Cm0 was not as large as had been thought'. There were difficulties measuring in a wind tunnel 'where the small differences of two large quantities had to be taken'. It was proposed to fit a larger tailplane to improve stability for the later tests. High-speed tests would not be attempted until the larger tailplane was fitted. Hayne Constant (who had been working with Dr Griffith at the RAE) reported that the engine would not be available this year. R. McKinnon Wood, drawing attention to the advantages of sweepback, felt that the Miles E.24/43, which was already out of date, should be discontinued. The Chairman, Ben Lockspeiser, ruled that the E.24/43 should proceed on the same priority. He felt that the pilotless rocket aircraft would be the obvious way to carry out flight experiments as soon as possible. At the last meeting it had been decided that the programme should be in three stages: (1) small pilotless expendable aircraft; (2) small pilotless controlled aircraft; (3) larger piloted aircraft. Barnes Wallis felt that a plastic rocket, weighing about 600lb, would be the most suitable unit for the first proposal and would give 500lb thrust for a period of two minutes. This rocket would fit into a 3/10 scale model of the E.24/43 which would be about 8.6ft in overall length and about 8.1ft span. A Mach number of about 1 in level flight would probably be achieved. After discussion about their construction and design it was agreed the models should be expendable. A contract for 24 rocket-propelled models of the E.24/43 would be placed with Barnes Wallis who was Assistant Chief Designer, Aviation Section of Vickers. A suggestion that an aircraft be fitted with a jet propulsion engine was considered; 'it was agreed that sufficient data was not yet available to assess the relative advantages of jet, duct and pure rocket propulsion'. Ben Lockspeiser would write to Power Jets for a progress report and a target date when the engine would be available for fitting in an aircraft.

7 August   The Ministry of Aircraft Production merges with the Ministry of Supply to become the Ministry of Supply and Aircraft Production, under John Wilmot, the former Minister of Supply.

14 August

Twenty-sixth meeting of the Supersonic Committee. Barnes Wallis stated that a price for the rocket-propelled aircraft had been submitted; The Chairman, Ben Lockspeiser, asked for contract action 'to be urged'.

After discussion of a report by Ronald Smelt on 'German activities at Focke-Wulf' it was agreed that a report summarising the work the Germans had been doing should be prepared by Ronald Smelt with R. McKinnon Wood's collaboration.

A meeting on 30 July 'had cleared all the outstanding problems on E.24/43 save that of pilot's escape. Research into pilot ejection was now being energetically tackled for the second aircraft, whilst it was proposed to limit the speed of the first aircraft to some 360mph'.

'There was a long discussion on a power plant for a jet-propelled E.24/43 replacement. Messrs Constant and Griffith agreed that if research was started now the best motor available at any given time would incorporate a ducted fan and re-heat. But Dr Griffith said that if a motor was ordered in a year's time the plain jet would be superior to any ducted fan engine which could then be built from scratch.'

After discussion about airframe design Ronald Smelt believed that a motor giving 1,500lb thrust at ground level per sq ft of frontal area should be aimed at. It was generally felt that such a project could cruise at around 1,000mph. Power Jets would be asked to undertake the necessary development work.

September

Bell Aircraft respond to another USAAF specification that expressed their interest in investigating the high-speed flight characteristics and aerodynamics of a swept-wing configuration. They submit a new rocket-powered design, with a 40-degree swept-wing triple sonic dual rocket-powered airplane, constructed of heat-resistant alloys.

11 September

Twenty-seventh meeting of the Supersonic Committee. Barnes Wallis 'stated that the model of the E.24/43 incorporating the 12 five-inch rockets was being designed at Vickers. Later it was agreed that six of the models should have the original smaller tailplane to investigate the effect on stability; the modified larger tailplane would be fitted to the other eighteen models.

H.F. Vessey stated 'that the position with regard to the pilot's possibility of escaping from the E.24/43 in case of difficulty was not at all satisfactory. At the moment it appeared unlikely that development of explosive charges would be sufficiently advanced to provide means of freeing the cabin from the first aircraft and it might, therefore, be necessary to restrict flight to very slow speeds. RAE considered that the pilot's difficulties of exit were considerably greater than from normal high-speed fighters and that, only if the pilot could turn the aircraft upside down, would there be a reasonable chance of escape. It was considered that a year would be required to develop a method using explosive charges to cut the cabin and controls free so that the pilot could escape normally when the cabin had slowed down sufficiently'.

Ronald Smelt said that 'the possibility of pilot ejection complete with special seat at high speeds had been investigated' successfully. This method of escape might be adopted for future designs; there was no room for the necessary equipment in the E.24/43. The Chairman said 'it was clear the aircraft could not be expected to fly until the question of escape had been cleared'.

17 September   Letter to Power Jets from Ben Lockspeiser, re Engine Research for Supersonic Flight: 'With reference to discussions at my Supersonic Committee, it is requested that an item be added to Power Jets' research programme to cover the research required to provide an engine suitable for an aircraft developed from the Miles E.24/43. Flight at speeds up to say $1.5 \times$ the speed of sound may be envisaged and the view has been expressed that a motor giving 1,500lb thrust per sq ft of frontal area (at ground level) should be aimed at. Mr Constant has been present at these discussions and is aware of the objective we have in mind. We shall be glad to have your comment and proposals in due course. The matter should be treated as 'A' priority.'

1945

9 October	Twenty-eighth meeting of the Supersonic Committee. A letter from Power Jets confirmed that the development of an engine giving at ground level 1,500lb thrust per sq ft of frontal area had been added to their research programme. H.F. Vessey 'stated that the latest tunnel tests, which had not yet been published, showed that the pilot could only leave the E.24/43 safely if he could invert it. This was equally true at low or high speeds. Means of pilot ejection was being developed but would not be ready for the first machine. The arguments for and against continuing to build the aircraft were then recapitulated by the meeting. Finally Sir Melvill-Jones said that it was inconceivable that, in England, a man should be sent up in an experimental aircraft from which there was no escape in case of emergency, and the Chairman agreed that the whole question must be reconsidered in the light of this new information.'
	The Department of Scientific Research would 'reconsider whether construction of E.24/43 should continue'.
13 November	Twenty-ninth meeting of the Supersonic Committee. There was discussion on the design of the model rocket-propelled aircraft. Mr Vessey 'reported that a recent meeting had decided that the pilot's escape from the E.24/43 could be satisfactorily covered by cabin jettisoning alone as it was impossible to fit pilot ejection to reduce the risk in the low flying case without extensive redesign. Miles Aircraft were proceeding, with the collaboration of MoS experts from ARD, to design the necessary modifications to the aircraft.'
by December	Power Jets have developed the W.2/700 engine, plus the No. 4 Augmentor, to give a thrust of 6,950lb at 1,000mph at 36,000ft on a cold day with an air temperature of 10°C below ICAN.
3 December	Eric Brown makes first aircraft carrier landing of a pure jet aircraft, a Vampire, on HMS *Ocean*.
14 December	Contract signed by Bell for design and construction of two X-2s supersonic experimental aircraft for the USAAF.

27 December	Bell complete the first X-1 airframe, incorporating none of the design features of the Miles M.52.

1946

8 January	Thirtieth meeting of the Supersonic Committee. There was detailed discussion about the design of the model rocket-propelled aircraft and the dropping aircraft. It was reported that work on the jettisonable cabin for the E.24/43 was proceeding. Tunnel and blower tunnel tests were being made at RAE and Armament Research Department was co-operating on cutting charges. The Chairman, Dr Ben Lockspeiser, ruled that the standing item on the E.24/43 replacement should be deleted from the Agenda.
19 January	First flight of Bell X-1 as a glider at Pinecastle, Florida.
22 January	Whittle sends Roxbee Cox (the Chairman) letter of resignation from the Board of Power Jets (R & D) Ltd.
22 January	Memorandum from D of C(P) to Norbert Rowe re Contract No. SB.27157/C 23(c). 'The above contract, covering the supply of prototype aircraft to Spec. E.24/43 and additional bare airframes etc., was placed with Miles Aircraft on 13th December 1943 as a matter of urgency, but the progress so far made does not seem to have been very rapid. The firm have spent £73,000 to 30th November 1945, and estimate that it will cost at least £250,000 to complete. In these circumstances, you may wish to reconsider the project; if it is decided that it should continue, will you please obtain additional financial approval on the basis of the above estimate of final cost.'
24 January	Whittle sends Air Marshal Sir Alec Coryton, CRD (at MoS), letter of resignation. Power Jets remains in being as a small patent-holding company.
25 January	First unpowered flight of a Bell X-1, launched from a modified Boeing B-29 with Bell test pilot, Jack Woolams.

1946

12 February

Thirty-first meeting of the Supersonic Committee. Detailed discussion about the design, dropping site and parent aircraft for the model rocket-propelled aircraft was followed by discussion of Power Jets memorandum 'Intake Ducting for Supersonic Flight'. H.F. Vessey stated that 'the Contracts branches had questioned whether it was justifiable to continue to build the E.24/43 in view of the latest cost estimates'. The original three aircraft were to have been built for £100,000. Subsequently a test fuselage for Power Jets had been added at a cost of £30,000. It was now estimated that the contract would cost at least £250,000 to complete. The Chairman summarised his reasons for feeling that the work should stop. When the design was commenced even less was known of supersonic problems than at the time of speaking. The performance would not be as good as had been hoped. There was, moreover, apparently insuperable difficulty in assuring the safety of the pilot; servicing problems were also considerable. To go ahead would, he thought, be to make secondary results – the development of an engine with afterburning and an all-moving tailplane – unjustifiably important. Several speakers amplified his remarks, Dr Hawthorne making the case for continuing the work to provide an engine test bed and the Chairman said that the feelings of the meeting would help MAP to come to a decision.

13 February

Memorandum from H.F. Vessey to Air Cdre G. Silyn Roberts, Dr H.M. Garner and Sir Ben Lockspeiser. 'A decision on whether the E.24/43 is to be continued is requested. The matter was raised at DGSR's Supersonic Committee on 12.2.46 but no firm decision was reached. The opinion of the Committee was unanimous that there was no case for continuing on the grounds of obtaining information at transonic or supersonic speeds. A case was, however, put forward for the completion of the aircraft for use as a test bed of the engine. This engine was developed specially for the E.24/43 and, although it is not one in which we are seriously interested, it is an engine on which useful information on ducted fans and afterburning could be obtained. A decision on continuing with the E.24/43 appears to depend on:

(a) Whether a large expenditure on testing the engine is justified, and if (a) is agreed

(b) Whether the use of the E.24/43 as a test bed is the best and cheapest means of obtaining the required information.

Even if (a) is agreed there will be a considerable difficulty in using the E.9/44 [Note: the E.9/44 was the Armstrong Whitworth A.W.52 not the correct aircraft.] as a test bed for which it is essentially unsuited. The aircraft was designed purely for supersonic investigations and the space available for instrumentation is extremely limited. In addition, engine accessibility is very poor indeed. Considerable development is required to make the aircraft fly even at low speeds and the main outstanding points are:

(i) *Pilot's escape.* Pilot ejection and jettisonable cabin are considered necessary to give the pilot a reasonable chance of escape in the case of difficulties at low and high altitudes respectively. Pilot ejection is impossible without a serious re-design involving cost outside the present estimate and we were forced to agree to a jettisonable cabin only. The main problems of its design have yet to be solved.

(ii) *Power operation.* Bench tests of the power operation system to be fitted to all flying controls have been promising, but considerable development is required. Power operation is necessary for the speeds required for the engine tests unless the controls are re-designed.

(iii) *Landing speed.* The landing speed is very high and outside our present experience. A long runway will be essential but even with this SME Dept. RAE foresee the possibility of undercarriage failure due to sticking under the large horizontal and vertical loads which will occur. German experience with the Me 262 has shown this to be a real danger.

The firm's estimate is 'at least £250,000' to complete. This represents a future expenditure of at least £150,000. Past experience with the firm, particularly on the E.24/43, leads us to regard this as an under-estimate. Some expenditure could certainly be saved by reducing the number of aircraft from three to two or even one, but as the major problems are concerned with getting the first aircraft to fly satisfactorily, the saving would not be substantial.

If flight tests on the engine are essential, it is seriously suggested that less expense, and probably quicker results, would be obtained by designing and building a fresh aircraft on more conventional lines.

15 February   Memorandum from Air Cdre G. Silyn Roberts to Dr H.M. Garner and Sir Ben Lockspeiser: 'I advise that the contract for E.24/43 aircraft should be cancelled. Since the specification for this aeroplane was written, considerable additional information has been acquired and the technique of telemetering has developed into a practical proposition so that many of the problems of supersonic flight appear to be capable of solution by model tests which will be cheaper than full-scale tests and which will not involve risks of fatal accidents.

The aircraft would appear to be an expensive test bed for the engine and an unsatisfactory one also. The flying risks are high at low speeds and unknown at high speeds.

I should judge that the additional £150,000 required to finish this aeroplane could be better spent on making an aircraft which would be more suitable as an engine test bed if it is decided that the testing of this engine in the air is absolutely essential.'

18 February   Memorandum from Dr H.M. Garner to Sir Ben Lockspeiser: 'I agree with minutes 40 and 41 that the Contract should be cancelled.

It is unfortunate that we shall have no means of testing the engine. I do not consider that the building of a special aircraft for this would be justified. If we could get the B.M.W. plant from Munich we should have a suitable solution.

The file does not give a very clear picture of how the aircraft was born and of its early history. The Supersonics Committee has been directly interested in the aircraft, and its advice, and that of the RAE in detail, has been available throughout.

Although we had the best scientific advice in the country we made two bad mistakes (at least) in the design. These were the square wings and the annular intake. We found from German information in 1945 of the great advantage of swept-back wings and recent experiments have shown that the annular intake has low efficiency at high speeds. This information came to light nearly two years after the project was launched.

The effort spent has not all been wasted. We know something about the construction of thin bi-convex wings and through the successful tests of the Falcon about the behaviour of such wings at low speeds.'

20 February Handwritten minute to Air Cdre G. Silyn Roberts from Sir Ben Lockspeiser: 'We must cut our losses and cancel the contract on this aircraft. The matter was fully discussed at the last meeting of the Supersonic Cte and I have subsequently discussed the matter with the firm. There will be no tears anywhere except perhaps at PJs [Power Jets] – but we are not paying £250,000 to test an engine.

I believe the conception behind the decision to build this aircraft was to get supersonic information. We now know that was putting the cart before the horse. No more supersonic aircraft till the rocket-propelled models and wind tunnels have given us enough information to proceed on a reliable basis.'

27 February Memorandum to Air Cdre G. Silyn Roberts from Gp Capt G.E. Watt (Deputy Director, Turbine Experimentation and Chairman of the Gas Turbine Collaboration Committee):

1   'I have noted the previous minutes and it does not seem to be generally realised that the W.2/700 engine has already been tested most adequately in the air, in fact it is still the best altitude engine of the Whittle series including those made by Rolls-Royce, and all the good features in this engine have been incorporated by Messrs Rolls-Royce in the Derwent V – the engine used for the record breaking Meteor. Therefore there is no need to worry about providing a test bed for this particular engine.

1946

2   However, a large amount of material will be scrapped because the W.2/700 engine was only to be the prime mover; – there was an extensive system of ducted fans with low pressure loss combustion which was to be used to give a large increase in thrust when required. Already a considerable amount of test work has been done, and although something has been learned which will be of general use, it is a pity that Power Jets (R & D) Ltd., who have only a limited capacity should have been prevented from tackling many of the other important problems of their programme, by encouraging them to go on with this M.52 project which is now to be dropped before realisation.

3   I am concerned especially on this point because I do not think it is generally realised that in order to clear a new engine for flight we almost invariably spend more money than is spent on the manufacture of the prototype aircraft which is to take the engine and therefore I am really making a plea for careful planning in order to husband our very slender resources.

4   In anticipation that the contract on Miles will be cancelled, we will suspend the work at Power Jets which applies to this particular project and will then review the whole question of supersonic engines at the next programme meeting.'

12 March   Thirty-second meeting of the Supersonic Committee. Barnes Wallis reported that work on the 'model of the models for the RAE tunnel tests was well in hand. If priority could be assured for the manufacturers the first model should be ready in two to three months'.

13 March   Miles Aircraft receive letter of cancellation; all work is stopped and a directive from the MoS instructs that the hardware, drawings, photographs, reports, etc., produced by Miles in conjunction with the M.52 project should be disposed of within a month.

15 May   First flight of the tailless fixed-slots de Havilland DH108 by Geoffrey de Havilland.

June	First flight of second DH108 (with lockable automatic slats) by Geoffrey de Havilland.
1 July	Power Jets (R & D) Ltd formally converted to National Gas Turbine Establishment (NGTE). Flight Testing Unit taken over by the newly constituted National Gas Turbine Establishment.
8 July	Second American visit to Miles Aircraft takes place, with Major E.N. Hall and Major Kent Parrot of the Air Technical Section of the Military Intelligence Division. They reported: 'The Miles M.52 is a bullet nosed, mid wing, jet-propelled supersonic design on which Miles has laboured for about two years. The construction contract was cancelled by M.O.S. at the end of June [the project was actually cancelled in March 1946], apparently because it was thought that several details of the project, while still feasible, had now become obsolete. The turbo-jet power plant, for instance, is an early model of comparatively low thrust and the induction system seems to leave much to be desired. The firm now has all jigging and tooling completed and about 90% of all airframe components fabricated, but not assembled for Model No. 2. Model No. 1 was completed and destroyed in a series of satisfactory static tests. A program of unmanned telemetered flights by a series of small models to be constructed by Vickers, as envisaged in the original plan, will still be performed. It is the opinion of this office that the firm may complete the M.52 on its own when its financial atmosphere becomes more propitious. It could be finished within a month, etc., etc.'

The report concluded: 'Other pertinent information on the efficiency of this system is expected to be yielded by the telemetered trials of the Vickers Supersonic model. These were designed by Miles as part of the M.52 project.' (In fact, they were designed by Barnes Wallis at Vickers but were based on the design of the Miles M.52.)

The report was signed by John S. Griffith, Colonel, Air Corps, Asst. Military Air Attache, Chief, Air Section. It confirms the exact position as to the state of the two prototype aircraft at the time of the cancellation and even what actually happened to the first prototype, which had been the subject of much speculation over the years.

1947

September	Thirteen months after new government took over and six months after its cancellation Miles are allowed to reveal the existence of the M.52 and the fact that it had been cancelled.
27 September	Second DH108, preparing for an airspeed record attempt, crashes into Thames estuary, killing the pilot Geoffrey de Havilland. The research aircraft, built to investigate the behaviour of swept wings and a tailless layout, suffered structural failure at high subsonic speed.
9 December	Bell makes first rocket flight of second prototype of the X-1 with Chalmers Goodlin as the pilot. The X-1 climbed to 35,000ft and achieved a speed of Mach.75/510mph.

1947

17 January	Bell reach a Mach number of 0.82 with second prototype of the X-1.
10 April	Bell recommence glide flight testing.
29 May	Bell conclude its flight demonstrations with the second prototype of the X-1.
30 May	First attempt to launch rocket model of the M.52 (model A-1), as part of Operation *Neptune*. Aircraft loses control at height and model falls off before it can be launched.
5 June	Bell completes the contractor's flight demonstration programme after a total of nine glide flights on the first prototype of the X-1. Plane handed over to the USAAF to start the programme leading to supersonic flight.
6 August	USAAF conducts its first glide flight of the X-1, flown by Chuck Yeager who carries out 23 flights between August 1947 and April 1948.
25 September	Yeager flies acceptance flight on the second prototype of the X-1 on behalf of NACA.
8 October	Second test of the rocket-powered M.52 model, made out of St Eval in Cornwall is unsuccessful – motor explodes! Attempts over the following twelve months to launch a rocket model are unsuccessful.

1948

early October	On sixth flight Yeager loses control of the X-1, flying at M=0.94 at 40,000ft.
14 October	On seventh flight, after 'flying tail' has been fitted to the X-1, Yeager attains controlled supersonic level flight, Mach 1.02 (date stage managed to herald the founding of USAF and demise of USAAF).
21 November	First supersonic jet, North American XP-86, flown by George Welsh, achieves Mach 1.02 and 1.03 in dives.
December	Study contracts placed for supersonic research aircraft:
	(a) three prototype English Electric P.1 research aircraft with swept wings and (b) two Fairey Delta 2 delta-winged research aircraft. First flights of the aircraft will be made in 1954.
	The specification for the P.1 prototypes shared a number of innovations first planned for the M.52, including the shock cone and all-moving tailplane or stabilator. They were built to the 1947 MoS Operational Requirement ER.103 for a transonic research aircraft; the chief designer was W.E.W. 'Teddy' Petter.

1948

10 March	Herbert Hoover, NACA test pilot, flying the Bell X-1 became the first civilian to fly supersonically.
9 September	High-speed DH108, flown by DH chief test pilot John Derry, makes first British supersonic flight in an uncontrolled dive from 40,000 to 30,000ft.
10 October	The last of the Vickers models of the M.52, as part of Operation *Neptune*, launched successfully from a Mosquito at about 400mph at 36,400ft, west of St Mary's in the Isles of Scilly. Model reaches a speed of 934mph, Mach 1.38, following a 55-second burn and flies on for approximately 90 miles. Contract immediately cancelled as being too expensive. The M.52 costs, including cancellation costs, have been estimated at £166,000 – a saving of £84,000 of the estimated £250,000 completion price. The subsequent rocket model programme, Operation *Neptune*, cost around £500,000.

1956

1950	
1 April	Two flying prototypes and one static test-frame of the English Electric P.1A ordered for evaluation.
Nov–Dec	Two examples of X-2 airframe completed but without rocket engines. The X-2 apparently incorporates several of the Miles M.52 design features: a bi-convex airfoil, all-moving tailplane and an escape pod.
1954	
4 August	Maiden flight of English Electric P.1A research aircraft from Boscombe Down: pilot Roland Beamont.
11 August	On its third flight, flown by Beamont, the P.1A became the first British aircraft to exceed the speed of sound in level flight – Mach 1.02 – at an altitude of 30,000ft.
October	Maiden flight of Fairey Delta 2 research aircraft.
1955	
February	Conservative Government publish White Paper 'The Supply of Military Aircraft' in which it condemns the cancellation of the M.52 which it says 'seriously delayed the progress of aeronautical research in the UK'.
October	Fairey Delta 2 makes its first supersonic flight.
18 November	First powered flight of the X-2 reaches speed of Mach 0.95 (627mph).
1956	
10 March	Fairey Delta 2, flown by Peter Twiss, achieves a world record of 1,132mph (Mach 1.73) – 30% greater than the American-held record. The record was next broken in December 1957, by a USAF McDonnell JF-101A Voodoo.
23 July	Ninth powered flight of the X-2 establishes an unofficial world speed record, with a speed of Mach 2.8706/1,900.34mph.

Bibliography

Books

Amos, Peter: *Miles Aircraft – The Early Years* (Air Britain, 2009: ISBN 978-0-85130-410-6)

– *Miles Aircraft – the Wartime Years* (Air Britain, in preparation)

– *Miles Aircraft – the Postwar Years* (Air Britain, in preparation)

Brown, Captain Eric: *Wings on My Sleeve* (Weidenfeld & Nicolson, 2006: ISBN hardback 978-0-2978-4565-2; paperback 978-0-7538-2209-8)

Golley, John: *Whittle – the true story* (Airlife, 1996: ISBN 0-906393-82-5)

Hallion, Richard P.: *Supersonic Flight* (Collier-Macmillan, 1972)

Hamilton-Paterson, James: *Empire of the Clouds – When Britain's Aircraft Ruled the World* (Faber & Faber, 2010: ISBN 978-0-571-24794-3)

Kempel, Robert W.: *The Conquest of the Sound Barrier* (X-Planes Book 7, HPM Publications, 2007)

Whittle Sir Frank: *Jet – the Story of a Pioneer* (Frederick Muller, 1953)

Wood Derek: *Project Cancelled* (Indianapolis, 1975: ISBN 978-0672521669)

Articles and Papers

Bancroft, D.S.: The Mystery of the Cancellation of the Miles M.52 (E.24/43) Contract by the Ministry of Supply in March 1946, December 1997

Brinkworth, B.J.: On the aerodynamics of the Miles M.52 (E.24/43) – a historical perspective, *The Aeronautical Journal*, March 2010

High Speed Research, *The Aeroplane Spotter*, 19 October 1946

McDonnell, Patrick: Beaten to the Barrier, *Aeroplane Monthly*, January 1998

Miles on Supersonic Flight: Background of M.52 Development: Design Problems Analysed, *Flight*, 3 October 1946

Our Supersonic Progress, *The Aeroplane*, 9 May 1947

Index

scale test models 57, 58, 59, 60, 109,
166–172
specification E24/43 21, 23, 36, 38, 82, 92,
132, 187, 189, 195, 197, 198, 199, 202,
203, 205, 206
Vickers rocket-propelled models 84, 91, 92,
104, 113–8, 133, 134, 160, 165, 172, 195,
196–7, 198, 199, 202, 203, 204, 208, 209,
210–1
wings 29, 33, 34, 35, 36, 38, 40, 41, 47,
52–3, 54, 63, 81, 82, 89, 90, 109, 110, 111,
154–5, 157, 158, 166, 167, 170, 184, 185,
186, 189, 192, 193, 207
Ministry of Aircraft Production (MAP) 21,
34, 36, 62, 94, 98, 129–30, 144, 178, 187,
199, 204
Ministry of Supply (MoS) 65, 100, 101, 102,
120, 129, 199
Ministry of Supply and Aircraft Production
130, 132, 140, 199, 208
Mitchell, R.J. 13, 14
ML Aviation 58
Montagnon, P.E. 187
Morgan, Morien 45, 60, 96, 100, 141
Multhopp, Professor 112

N

National Advisory Committee for
Aeronautics (NACA) 62, 63, 118, 177, 184,
194, 196, 210, 211
Muroc Flight Test Unit 118
National Gas Turbine
Establishment (NGTE) 99, 111, 209
National Physical Laboratory (NPL) 27, 28,
30, 34, 58, 60, 156, 169, 170, 176, 177, 181,
186, 187, 190, 195

Nelson, Sqn Ldr Jimmy 43
North American Mustang 45, 181, 184
North American XP-86 supersonic jet 211
Northrop YB-49 bomber 95

O

Ocean, HMS 202
Operation *High Ball* 90
Operation *Neptune* 210, 211

P

Parrot, Major Kent 65, 192, 209
Petter, W.E.W. 'Teddy' 211
Phillips and Powis Aircraft Ltd 23, 178
Power Jets Limited 30, 32, 34, 40, 41, 42, 67,
68, 69, 73, 74, 75, 81, 96, 98, 99, 100, 102,
110, 128, 156, 163, 168, 176, 177, 178, 179,
185, 187, 188, 190, 191, 196, 198, 201, 202
Power Jets (Research and Development)
Limited 129, 130, 131, 132, 133, 142, 188,
203, 204, 207, 208, 209
Pugsley, Dr 180
Putt, Colonel Donald 148

R

RAE Transonic Research Aircraft 112
Relf, Ernest 27, 28, 29, 181, 187
Republic Thunderbolt 45
Roberts, Air Cdre G. Silyn 160, 204, 206, 207
Rolls-Royce Limited 98, 99, 192, 207
Rose, Tommy 93
Rowe, Norbert E. 23, 34, 35, 78, 156, 157,
177, 178, 179, 180, 181, 182, 184, 185, 186,
187, 198, 203
Royal Aircraft Establishment, Farnborough
(RAE) 14, 17, 18, 21, 23, 27, 28, 33, 34, 36,